OUR SHAWNEE

OUR SHAWNEE

BY

PRECIOUS BARNETT

CALLIE COMER

ASIA FREY

CODY HARRAL

DAVID McCONICO

JODECI THOMAS

DEVANTE URBINA

TAYLOR "NALA" WINEMILLER

EDITED BY BRIAN WEINBERG AND DARCY THOMPSON

LOUISVILLE STORY PROGRAM

Paper, printing, and binding provided at cost by
Publishers Printing Company, Shepherdsville, KY, USA

ISBN 978-0-9914765-0-3

Library of Congress Control Number: 2014937227

Book design by Shellee Marie Jones
Cover photograph by Nala Winemiller
Back cover photograph by Wesley Bacon / Kertis Creative

CONTENTS

INTRODUCTION

In the spring of 2013, the Louisville Story Program partnered with The Academy @ Shawnee to offer all members of the school's junior class the opportunity to participate in an extracurricular writing project. Eight students living in Louisville's West End—specifically in Shawnee, Portland, Iroquois, and Algonquin—were excited by the idea of publishing their stories in a professionally designed book, and brave enough to trust LSP as we were conducting our first-ever project.

Earning a paycheck for their participation, they spent the summer in writing workshops led by LSP staff and other professional writers and journalists. They read great literary nonfiction and did writing exercises to learn about craft, working their way through a college-level creative writing curriculum. They also received training in oral history interview techniques, and spent many hours in the field with digital recorders conducting participatory, community-based research—interviewing family members, friends, and neighbors.

The writing of their book chapters was emotionally taxing at points throughout the process. Authors delved into their past, sometimes writing about painful topics. At times they struggled through writer's block and self-doubt, and they encountered a number of outside challenges and potential distractions. But they persevered. Throughout the fall of 2013 and into early 2014, authors met with LSP staff in classrooms after school, in public libraries, at home, and in coffee shops. They also took photographs in their neighborhoods with the assistance of professional photographers and sourced photographs from family albums to accompany their stories.

Finally, after countless hours of re-writes, editing, follow-up interviews, and soul searching, the book that you are holding now came into existence. Each author's chapter consists of three parts: (1) a brief descriptive prose piece about his or her neighborhood, (2) a longer literary essay on a subject of personal importance, and (3) a shaped interview with the questions removed, presented as first-person narration from the interviewee.

The writers you are about to read—Asia, Callie, Cody, David, Devante, Jodeci, Nala, and Precious—undertook this project not only in the interest of personal growth, but in the spirit of building a better community, to help promote dialogue across Louisville. We hope that this book conveys what we have come to appreciate so deeply: these young authors are extraordinary people with a lot to teach us.

Darcy Thompson and Brian Weinberg
Louisville Story Program
www.louisvillestoryprogram.org

CALLIE COMER

Lytle Street, Portland

Not Quite Betty Crocker

Those Damn Cheap Tissues

LYTLE STREET, PORTLAND

From the porch of my shotgun house, I can see the spire of Shawnee Baptist Church, white with a cross, much like every other church of the Christian faith. It peeks over the rooftops and glows in the warm setting sun. On the porch of the house next door is a Coke machine filled to the brim, only fifty cents per can. The neighbor is a good man with a long braid and scruffy beard, and he's taught me many things, like how to use electric trimmers on my brother's hair, and to spray-paint to the can's full potential when making art.

Across the street is an auto shop with loud roaring cars that speed down Lytle at all hours, annoying at times, but hey, at least the men are passionate about something. Near the shop is the back entrance to the Portland Museum, brick and vines on the outside, full of river-life history inside, a high-quality museum, though I hardly ever see any visitors.

PHOTOS BY CALLIE COMER

Farther down is the house with many cats, renovated with a new walkway and porch. Far from a crazy cat lady, the woman who lives there is sweet and sociable, often giving me cheese to give to my aunt as a thank you for finding her lost kittens. Farther still is the McDonald's where kids from my school work, and where my mom worked for a brief time. I sometimes go there for breakfast before school and do my makeup in the ladies room. Men sit in the booths, coffee in hand, some with laptops for the free Wi-Fi.

Beyond my street lie daycares and banks that I've never been in, and a Circle K where I proudly take up the profession of professional loiterer, chatting about horror flicks and anime with the guys who work the late shift. Off in the distance, the downtown skyline is prettiest during the holiday season, especially at night. Bright reds and greens atop the buildings, the lights of cold nights and the Light Up Louisville festival.

Back on my porch, the weather is still warm: bright blooming flowers, singing metallic wind chimes, and my neighbor's smile that seemingly never leaves, just like the old shotgun houses and ancient trees of Portland, a neighborhood I've come to know as home. ■

NOT QUITE BETTY CROCKER

There was a time when I didn't know that the words "drugs" and "Mom" went together.

My mother was a beautiful young woman named Christy, wide at the hips with flowing brown hair, bright brown eyes and a full smile. She got along with most everyone and had a fun nightlife. She'd go to Phoenix Hill on Bardstown Road to see shows, or to the Portland Post to see her friends play in a band called 99MPH. She had cool clothes, a sense of rebellious style. I especially loved her T-shirt for the nu-metal band Korn. "I have issues," it stated.

Her arms were covered with scars from cigarettes being extinguished on her skin, which didn't seem like an issue to me as a little girl. She had scars on her back from incense being hot-glued to her skin and then lit. She used to try to hide drugs and paraphernalia from my younger brother Logan and me. Silly tricks like putting a lampshade on top of a bong and saying it was a lamp. She'd make us watch movies while she joined our Uncle Bub in the kitchen for "grownup time." When I was about six, I busted in on them, accidentally. He was cutting up green stuff—I didn't know what pot looked like—and screamed, "Get out!"

I knew from then on.

Mom gave birth to me at sixteen and was more into partying than changing diapers. "I'm not no Betty Crocker cookie-cutter mom," she'd say. My father was mostly absent, didn't participate in my upbringing. For part of my childhood, I lived with my grandma, whom we called Nanny. Only in her forties, Nanny didn't like to be called Grandma. Mom worked at Subway in those days, and would crash at Uncle Bub's house at night. One morning, she stopped by Nanny's on her way to work to say hi to Logan and me. It was almost her birthday, or it had just passed, and I decided to walk with her partway to the bus stop. It wasn't every day that she stopped by, and I wanted to stretch out our time as much as possible.

I noticed a piece of twisted metal on the sidewalk, masterfully shaped into the word "bitch," which, believe it or not, was a perfect birthday present for Mom. "Bitch," or rather "beyotch," was her nickname among friends. My heart swelled with joy when she affixed the metal to her backpack—my present displayed proudly for all to see—among the many buttons and patches, key chains of all types, safety pins of all sizes, beer bottle caps, and even a pink fishnet thong she'd gotten from a female performer at Phoenix Hill.

PHOTO COURTESY OF CALLIE COMER

Me as a live-action porcelain doll

I so admired that backpack, and her tattoos were really cool, too: the names of her kids in flowing script across her forearm, a Hello Kitty angel in the bend of her arm to honor her best friend's death, a cross at the nape of her neck, a rose above her butt cheek, a roundish tribal design on her chest, a star on her collarbone, a tiny black heart on her chest that Nanny had tattooed using a sewing needle and India ink, and a collage of eyeballs on her shoulder. She loved eyeballs so much. "Windows to the soul," she'd say.

I've been told that what started my mom's pill addiction was a trip to the dentist. She got a root canal and they gave her an insane amount of Xanax. But even as a child, she had an experimental, addictive personality. In middle school, she had to be rushed to the hospital after taking a handful of diet pills.

When Mom would run out of Xanax or Lortab, she'd be in so much pain that she'd cry. I imagined that she was so used to having her body numb from painkillers that the unmedicated feeling of her body "working" was too much for her. Heart pumping, stomach sloshing, muscle movement—those sensations were magnified, excruciating.

When she was on painkillers, she was either out of her mind with giddiness, giggling and joking, or deeply relaxed, falling asleep with a cigarette in her mouth. Her inhibitions and awareness went out the window. I can't count all the repetitive conversations we had, stories about her adventurous sex life and everything I had to "look forward to." Or how many times we'd go to rent movies and Mom would pick out a DVD she'd already seen, insisting she hadn't

seen it. She exposed me to disturbing but beautiful movies like *Gummo*, *Trainspotting*, and *Caligula*.

Aside from Boyz II Men and New Kids on the Block, I loved her musical taste. She was into Acid Bath, Tool, Pink Floyd. I can still see her on a comfy, worn couch, beer in hand, her eyes closed as she sways softly side to side, singing "Bleed Me an Ocean" by Acid Bath. Her voice isn't perfect, it doesn't match the tone or pitch, but she's happy. She sings, "Just like a raindrop/I was born, baby, to fall/And scale these prison walls." Then she opens her eyes and says, "F---, that is so beautiful!"

She had so much heart and passion singing those songs. Seemingly the only time she was truly deeply happy was in the company of a good song. Not that she didn't have lots of friends. She was popular. I called her pill-head friends "butterfly chasers." Not because they literally chased butterflies, but because they'd stop talking mid-sentence and do or say something completely random, as though it were the most important thing in the world, their eyes far away, half-lidded. Everything in a butterfly chaser's reality is a numb, confusing reality, a pocket of mind called memory that was long ago shut down.

■ ■ ■

In my family, the females suffer from depression, anxiety, health problems, chemical imbalances—it goes on and on. When I was in seventh grade, I came home to find Nanny keeled over dead on top of my newborn sister, Natalyn, who was crying in her baby carrier. I knew Nanny was dead and not passed out, not because of any physical signs, but because of an eerie feeling you get. Things seem to stand still when you come across a dead person. Then, a static roars around you as you start to panic. Brody, my baby brother, had just turned one, and was playing with toys off in the corner.

Nanny had health problems and was depressed after her husband died in his early forties. She always told me that if she keeled over not to call 9-1-1. I was torn, pacing back and forth, crying and scream-ing at her. I loved her so much and wanted the paramedics to try to resuscitate her, but Nanny didn't want to live anymore, and I didn't want her to be mad at me for calling an ambulance.

I tried to lay her out straight on the floor and give her CPR, but couldn't stop shaking. When I screamed next door to the neighbors, they came running into the house and took the babies outside, and then dragged me out also. Soon Mom showed up

and couldn't stop crying and apologizing for not being around when I needed help.

All four kids went to live with Mom. In those days, she was going to a methadone clinic to try to wean herself off pills. We had a silver Chevrolet Venture Warner Bros. edition van with automatic sliding doors and a VHS player. Every morning, Mom would wake us up and get Natalyn into her car seat, and then drive me to Western Middle School down in Portland. I'd try to keep an eye on her behind the wheel; she could get hazy from the methadone. One morning, after she dropped me off, she actually nodded off and smashed into a utility pole at the bottom of a hill. Thankfully, Natalyn was at home, in her car seat. Mom had forgotten to put her in the van. I had noticed this but said nothing, feeling moody.

I'd get so mad at Mom for her addic-tion problems and how she acted. But then again, I never wanted her to leave me unless she told me where she was going or what she was doing. One time, I was so worried that I stood in a pouring rainstorm for an hour, waiting for her to get home from work. Another time, when our food stamps were in, Mom and I took a trip to Kroger. She couldn't stop giggling and joking. I was doing the shopping with a grocery list I'd

PHOTO COURTESY OF CALLIE COMER

Mom and Cynthia, one of her oldest friends

made up myself, and she pushed the cart. Whenever I asked her to grab an item, she'd turn pouty and chuck the item into the cart, damaging the package.

At one point, I noticed her marveling at a bottle of ranch dressing. She held it up and asked, "Callie, can we get it?" She looked like a child, so hopeful, begging me with her big brown eyes. Before I could answer, she discovered a bigger bottle and said, "Wow! Look at how *big* this one is and only two dollars more." I felt like a mom, or at least what I assume a mom feels like. I told her to get the smaller bottle, and then went on shopping.

But she wasn't always so kooky on pills. She could be extremely aware. One night, I stood at the sink trying to do a week's worth of dishes. Old greasy food clung to plates, hard-as-rock Ramen Noodles stuck in bowls. I was scraping with a sponge, increasingly frantic, wanting to shatter every dish and storm out. Suddenly, warm tattooed arms embraced me from behind. Her cheek pressed against mine. I leaned back to return the hug as best I could with sudsy hands.

"Just thought you needed one," Mom said.

I appreciated moments like those, and that she was so nonjudgmental, at least compared to other mothers I knew. As a teenager, I never had to hide who I was deep down inside. Mom not only accepted my eccentricities, she celebrated them. She liked my spiked collars, goth makeup, and deep affection for drag queens. She'd help me with my hair and makeup, and ask to borrow my tops and jewelry when she'd go out at night, promising not to lose my belongings or spill beer on them. Mom was always looking for new things to expose me to, whether it was music, film, or lifestyle, and sometimes she included me in her counterculture adventures.

One of the coolest times we hung out was at a tenth anniversary party for a tattoo shop. I can't remember if Mom was on pills or a little drunk, but she was loopy. She'd heard about the party through her favorite tattoo artist, a man who had done some of the more breathtaking tattoos on her body.

I fell in love with the scene as soon as we pulled up. Outside the shop was a lady in a beautiful top hat announcing a raffle for top hats and demonic-looking dolls. Inside, large paintings of bold women and monsters were everywhere. There was also a five dollar sale on "666" tattoos, which perked Mom's interest big-time, but she bought me two raffle tickets instead, even though she was basically broke. She drank and socialized with different people, admiring their tattoos and showing off her own. I was happy to see her having fun for a change. She never looked so at home as when she was lounging back in that leather tattoo chair.

When I didn't win the raffle, I wasn't disappointed, but Mom sure was. She had an idea that I could trade some of my artwork for a top hat. I thought she was crazy, dragging me and my large folder of drawings to the hat maker. The woman was tiny, only a little taller than me, with pale skin and bright red lipstick. She wore a brown striped dress and seemed friendly. Mom did what she always did: brag on me. She told the woman how wonderful and creative my illustrations were, and I got two beautiful top hats in exchange for three drawings.

When the cops arrived due to loud techno music and fire dancers, everyone headed homeward. Mom had had a drink or three, and was loopier than when we arrived. The hat maker wanted us to call somebody to drive us home, but I assured her that everything was fine, feeling embarrassed. She said "okay" in a worried voice, and handed me her business card, saying that if Mom couldn't get us home that I should call her.

I rushed off to help Mom get behind the wheel of the van. She didn't pass out until I had her safely in the house. I saw the hat maker only one time after that. I called her up using the number on her card, and she had me over for dinner. She was so cool and sweet to me. But it was hard to build lasting friendships when my home life was so fickle. We lost touch.

■ ■ ■

When I was fourteen, Mom used a stun gun to tase herself about twenty times in a row. Believe it or not, this was to make Logan stop crying. A teenager named James was living with us; his mom was down on her luck, an addict also. He tased Logan in the back as a "joke."

Logan sat outside in the rain crying, waiting for Mom to get home. Of course Mom was furious that Logan had been tased against his will, but at the same time she thought Logan was crying too much. Getting tased "didn't hurt that bad," and to prove her point, she tased herself in the arms, neck, breasts, tummy—basically all over her body.

"Now Logan, you stop crying!" she shouted. "And James, don't tase my kid again!"

All James could do was stare, wide-eyed, and cover his mouth in pure shock. I was

My little brother Logan being a goofball

mortified too, and yet strangely sort of proud of her. Maybe it was her willingness to take extreme measures. Maybe she was showing her love, her anguish.

Our house could be loud and crazy like that. Sometimes I'd come home and just stand outside the front door, listening to all the yelling inside. After about ten minutes, I'd go in and close myself in my room for as long as I could. One day, I was belly-down on Mom's bed, watching disk three of the *Drawn Together* DVD set I'd borrowed from James, when there was a banging on the front door. Mom yelled for the knocker to come in, and I snuck down the hallway to investigate. Three looming cops and a worker from the housing authority stood in the living room. I turned on my heel and shut myself back in Mom's room. Whatever was happening, it wasn't going to lead to flowers and rainbows.

I tried to distract myself by watching cartoons. I knew we had a filthy house, holes punched in the walls, toys so thick on the floor you could no longer see the tile in Logan's room. To top it all off, Timmy, my mom's boyfriend and father to Brody and Natalyn, moseyed into the living room tearing a dime bag open with his teeth; he didn't know the police were there and almost got arrested for possession.

We had three hours to get our belongings out of the house and find a place to go. A seemingly impossible task was taken care of with three phone calls. First, a call to Amy, my mom's best friend and James's mother, to ask for an empty room to store our belongings—we didn't have much, just a couple of dressers and a gray and purple couch Mom and Timmy had just bought. Next, a call to my Aunt Teresa; my brother and I would need to stay with her so we could keep going to the same school while Mom went apartment shopping and sorted out the mess we were in. The final call was for transportation to move our stuff; our van had been repossessed. Fortunately, I was a member of a very supportive mentoring group in New Albany. They were at my house in twenty minutes to help us move.

Everything was going smoothly, and then things crashed again. I was helping load the couch into the back of a truck when I heard Timmy yelling at my Mom inside the house. I thought nothing of it until he poked his head out the door and screamed, "Callie, Christy's having a stroke!"

My mind went completely blank. Then I started walking, slowly, toward the house.

Mom was sprawled on the couch, her eyes half-lidded and glazed. She was foaming at the mouth, spitting and gasping, her body heaving in the air and falling again. I was terrified. There were two strangers in the house: a skinny dark-haired man and a chunky woman with pink hair. They were trying to help Timmy as best they could.

Timmy yelled at me to get a spoon and I didn't understand why. The only spoons we had were plastic, and without looking at it, he shoved it in Mom's mouth. Sure enough, she bit down and shattered the spoon. Timmy cursed, and while he was digging the pieces out of her mouth, she bit his finger.

"Christy, you bit my finger!" he yelled.

In all my panic and fear, I found this a little funny, because Mom didn't have any teeth. She'd had every tooth pulled after they rotted from the thick red poison known as methadone. The lady with pink hair told me to hold my mother's head up; her hair was sweaty, it tangled in my fingers. The pink-haired lady pointed to me and asked Mom, "Do you know who this is?" Mom's eyes slowly dragged to my face, and her eyebrows knitted together as she shook her head no.

"That's your daughter."

Now I wanted to cry. This wasn't the first time someone I loved dearly failed to recognize me. At maybe five years old, I hugged my favorite grandpa around his waist, but he didn't hug back. He looked down at me as though he'd never seen me before in his life. Dementia, most likely, but I took it personally, as if he didn't love me anymore.

Somebody called 9-1-1, and soon enough, the ambulance was there to take Mom away. She called me later that night while we were driving furniture to Amy's house. She said not to worry, everything was going to be fine. I wasn't so sure. Her bright eyes were dull and sad these days, like a basset hound's. She no longer wore her body jewelry, and small holes dotted her skin from the piercings. She no longer styled her hair, just pulled it all back into a bun and went about her day. She seemed to be running on fumes, just trying to hang on. She'd mentioned checking herself into the psychiatric ward at Floyd Memorial Hospital, near our house, but was afraid they'd never let her leave.

■ ■ ■

After living with my Aunt Teresa for a while, we moved to a single bedroom house next door to the Portland Museum on Portland Avenue. This was in the dead of winter, and we went without heat for several months. It's hard to sleep when it's too hot, but trying to sleep in pure cold is a torture all its own. Heat makes you irritable, while cold makes you feel much worse, like you're all alone, no matter how much you bundle up. There's always a draft biting you from somewhere, making you feel hopeless and worn out. It's a feeling that makes you want to cry, and sometimes I did.

Even though the ceilings and windows were tall, the house was tiny. Amy lived with us and was paying most of the rent; she'd lost her kids to Child Protective Services, and stayed in the bedroom with the queen-sized bed. I slept on a pile of blankets and pillows in the corner of Amy's room, under a chilly window. Timmy and the babies had mattresses in the living room. Logan, when he wasn't out with friends, slept on the couch. Mom would crash on the loveseat.

Sometimes I'd eat only once a day. School was my main source of food, but no one would ever guess it because Logan and I were chubby no matter how little we ate. Our diet consisted of SpaghettiOs, Ramen Noodles, pizza, McDonald's. Sometimes we had the ingredients to make chicken alfredo. We got food stamps on a regular basis, receiving as much as $800 a month, but it never mattered how much we saved because Mom would spend the money on

pills. At the beginning of each month, Mom bought us candy and food and pop, but by the middle of the month we were struggling. By the end of the month, we were almost starving.

Whenever I told Mom that we needed to put more money toward groceries, she'd tell me that no family needs $800 a month for food. Amy understood Mom's rationale. She'd get super-excited about scoring pills; she and Mom fed off each other's manic energy and self-destructive behavior.

Occasionally things happened that seemed so sad and pathetic we had to laugh. There was a small space heater that came with the house; it stayed in the living room with one broken wheel. One night, while we were eating dinner, it exploded. There was a flash of purple fire, and then it was over. All that remained was a busted heater and a scorched spot on the linoleum floor.

Eventually we were evicted due to missing rent payments. We stayed with Uncle Bub, an arrangement that lasted until I killed his goldfish with bleach that I was using to clean around the tank. I moistened the rag in the tank's water, not thinking. Funny, but not funny.

We stayed in a hotel on Dixie Highway at the beginning of our hotel-hopping spree.

There was a decent indoor pool, but we could only afford to stay one night. So we stole the pillows, which were big and fluffy, and headed to a cheaper hotel. Logan was staying with his friends in Portland, and the babies were at their grandma's, so it was just me, mom, and Timmy on this "grand" hotel adventure.

The next hotel was conveniently connected to a sex shop called Cirilla's. Every morning, Timmy would go off to one of his jobs—I never knew where he was working—and Mom and I would spend most of the day lugging boxes and garbage bags of our belongings from bus to bus. It was exhausting searching for a hotel every few days. I was always afraid of dropping a box.

We spent a few nights in a hotel that had a computer in the lobby, and I'd use the internet while Mom and Timmy got "alone time." In the morning, I'd go downstairs for the complementary breakfast and the local news. A friendly man with a greased pompadour told me all about Fear Fest, a horror-themed comic and movie convention that was taking place at the Galt House downtown. I really wanted Mom to take me, but we had to pack up and move on.

The next hotel was America's Best Inn, right off a highway exit. I'll always appreciate the irony of the worst hotels calling themselves things like America's Best Inn. It had a dirty outdoor pool attached to a bar and grill. The bathroom in our room was so tiny that it was hard to get into. It had no ventilation, so when you took a shower it slowly became harder and harder to breathe. Most of the guests treated this hotel like an apartment complex, staying for long stretches for a special low rate. Children ran the hallways, splashed in the pool, punched the vending machines, and hogged time on the crummy computer in the front lobby. Even the girl who worked behind the desk lived there. Her room was usually open, and I'd see her with a little girl, the two of them belly-down on the bed, watching cartoons.

Eventually, Brody and Natalyn came to stay, and our room became a disaster zone of toys and clothes. We'd take the kids to swim in the outdoor pool where older children splashed like idiots, and strange men stared at girls and boys alike. I was usually left alone to care for our little ones while Mom and Timmy ran errands. Every morning, I'd turn on Bubble Guppies for the kids and clean the destroyed room as best I could. Then I'd dress the kids and take them to get food from a gas station across the highway.

PHOTO COURTESY OF CALLIE COMER

My little siblings, Brody and "Natnat" (Natalyn)

It was scary to run across a busy highway with little kids. Even though I held their hands tightly, I imagined they would trip or break free.

One day, when Logan showed up to visit, he begged me to go night swimming. I refused, not wanting to deal with wet underclothes, but decided to sit out on the pool deck to keep an eye on him. A bloody fight broke out between two men.

This was my normal. It was frustrating. It was hopeless. I was such an angry person. I was always stressed out. Mom was telling us a story: we'd move to a nice little apartment, she'd get a steady job, keep the place clean, raise us kids right. A fresh start. I wanted to believe her, but couldn't.

■ ■ ■

It's nighttime. Our family of six is staying with friends in their broken-down house. It has no water and reeks of human waste. Mom is crying about being a bad mother, how we'd be better off without her. I tell myself she's trying her best. She tells me that she doesn't think she can make it much past her thirty-third birthday.

This I can believe. She's aging more and more every day. I know from my grandmother that the women in my family die around forty, so I've been trying to prepare myself for her death anyway. I tell her this, and she cries even harder. I feel like a mean person, but I have to prepare for these things.

Then Mom goes into the bathroom to soak in the tub. After an hour, the family we're staying with becomes aggravated and fidgety, needing to use the bathroom. I'm worried about my mother. Timmy is still at work, so I'm the only one who can check on her.

The door isn't locked. As I enter, it feels surprisingly cool, no fog on the mirror. Mom is passed out naked in the tub, which doesn't have any water in it. Stepping over piles of dirty clothes, I can see that her hair is damp. Droplets of water on her chest and shoulders. Then I notice blood. An open wound on the front of her shoulder, a bit larger than a quarter. Blood flows thinly down her arm. A razor blade is sitting on the tub's edge.

I grab her wrists, but no cuts there, or anywhere else that I can see. I shake her arm, tap her, call out her name. She tries to open her eyes, but can't. I'm answered with a groan.

"Mom, c'mon… are you okay? Mom, people gotta use it."

Trying to help her dress, I have trouble finding her clothes in the piles. Whenever I get her to cooperate, she suddenly snatches her clothes away from me, as if offended, and attempts to dress herself. It takes me over an hour of coaxing and waking her up to get her out of the bathroom and into bed.

The faces of the family are twisted in disapproval when I come back into the main room. They take turns using the bathroom. I flop down on the couch, amazed and exhausted. They speak in hushed voices about what Christy puts her family through. I say nothing, thinking, *If you guys are so concerned, why didn't you help me?*

■ ■ ■

It's extremely difficult writing about Mom. I can hear her voice, see her move in my mind. I want to see her alive again. Her smile, her eyes. I want her to hug me, kiss my forehead.

We're similar in so many ways. I laugh at inappropriate times and get excited over little ironies in the world, like that Wonka candy company came out with trippy-looking Mushroom Gummies marketed to kids. I'm very open-minded about sexuality and lifestyles. I dwell on the past, like she did. But I try to block out bad memories at the same time.

Like the day of Mom's death. Logan and I were at our Aunt Jenny's house because Mom was trying to find us another place to live. Mom had found out that Timmy was sneaking around with another girl. She was heartbroken and staying with Amy. When Jenny tried calling Mom to tell her that she'd gotten some mail, her expression turned grave. "You're kidding," she said. "We'll be right there."

She turned to us kids on the couch. "That was Amy. She thinks your mom is dead."

As we rushed to put on our shoes, I giggled. Who knows why. Maybe I always knew this day was coming, and here it was. Maybe I was going into shock. When we pulled up to Amy's yellow house on Bank Street, there was an ambulance parked in the driveway, and Amy was sitting casually on the white porch rail, her long skinny tattooed leg crossed over the other. She was smoking a cigarette, texting on her phone.

"Christy's inside," she told us flatly.

The paramedics wouldn't let anyone but Amy inside the house, which infuriated me. I asked Amy for Mom's phone so I could let my uncle know what was going on, and when she brought the phone outside I was confused—it wasn't Mom's phone, but a cheap replacement.

"Christy lost her phone last week at work or something," Amy explained.

Mom may have led a chaotic life, but she never lost her phone. I wondered what kind of craziness had been going on in her life. I wanted to call Payton, Amy's daughter and my best friend, but Mom's replacement phone kept exploding with incoming calls—friends and family who had already gotten word. I took the calls and explained that yes, Christy might be dead. I was still holding out hope that she might survive, but also knew that if she were still alive the paramedics would have rushed her away by now. People were shocked, people broke into tears. The more people I told, the less real it seemed, as if I couldn't believe my own words.

Eventually, Logan walked around the corner crying. He was fourteen years old.

PHOTO BY CALLIE COMER

Mama bear Jenny

I felt tears welling up also. Then it flashed in my head. What was I going to tell the babies? They were four and five, and they wouldn't understand. This made me start crying. It wasn't fair to them. Mom was so proud of them and loved them so much.

Soon the entire block was filled with people. Some I knew, some I didn't. Every five seconds I was embraced by a sobbing adult. They held onto me like a life raft, telling me how sorry they were. They were crying for themselves, they were crying for the loss of Christy, and they were crying for me and for my siblings, just as I had cried for the babies. What could I say? What could I say to comfort them?

■ ■ ■

There were a few people, including my Uncle Bub, who believed that Amy had given Mom the pills that killed her. He called her a "f---ing pill-head junky" when he showed up at her house. I'd always worried that it wasn't going to end well for Mom or Amy or both of them together. But no matter how much you worry and try to prepare yourself for the worst, it's still a shock when the worst actually happens.

When Timmy arrived with Brody and Natalyn, the babies simply didn't comprehend that their mother was dead. They played with the other children who happened to be around. It had only been a few weeks since Timmy had left Mom. When he gave me a hug, he felt bony but strong, and I realized that it was the first time we'd ever hugged in the six or seven years that I'd known him.

Eventually, the paramedics removed Mom's body from the house. She was covered in black. I followed Amy inside to retrieve Mom's purse. It was on the kitchen counter. I noticed a half-eaten Oatmeal Creme Pie on the floor, next to a large puddle of urine or drool, and realized that Mom had died right there on the cold green floor.

Then Amy's phone rang. She eagerly took the call, and I realized that she was setting up a pill run. I thought, *Really? Right after your best friend died from pills?*

She hung up and pointed to the puddle. "Look," she said.

Why would she point that out? Why would anyone do that? It felt like she was rubbing my face in my mother's death.

Back at Jenny's house, I texted the guy I was dating at the time. I received so many phone calls and messages on Facebook that I didn't know what to do with them all, and just ignored them. I appreciated that people were trying to check on me, but I was overwhelmed. Jenny suggested I take a shower to relax.

I stood under the warm water with a blank face and a blank mind. I didn't know what was going to happen to Logan and me in the long run, and I didn't much care. I wanted to wash the day away and relax. When I came back out to the living room, my boyfriend was sitting quietly on the couch. We didn't say much to each other. I leaned my head on his shoulder as we watched TV. All I wanted to do was zone out, but he was hungry and wanted to get food. So we set out and snacked around. Later, we reclined the seats in his car and watched YouTube videos.

■ ■ ■

It was a slow, sad ride to the funeral home. Logan, Jenny, and I squeezed into the backseat of Uncle Bub's car. Logan and I shared a headset and listened to upbeat music, his head on my shoulder. Ratterman & Sons Funeral Home was extremely good to us, offering as cheap a price as they could. Our family had been laid out in that home for generations. Heck, I'd grown up in the place.

I didn't care about the color of the coffin, I didn't care what was written in the obituary, and I didn't care who would be pallbearers. All the planning was stressful. The suggestion was made that I do Mom's makeup since I'd watched her apply her own makeup so many times. I wouldn't have minded, but the idea was quickly shot down because I wasn't a "qualified makeup professional."

Normally at funerals, I'd sit in the lounge with some coffee and engage in quiet conversation, but today, I had to go around the room accepting condolences. Every few minutes my worried and distraught uncle would rush up with panicked questions. Who are the pallbearers going to be? Who's that guy standing over there? Do you have the music?

Brody was dressed in a toddler suit, Natalyn in her Easter dress. They looked cute. When Amy showed up, her presence caused quite a stir. Angry glares and whispers. Everyone wanted her out, but nobody wanted to make a scene. And besides, my mother would've wanted her present.

When I went outside with Payton for some air, we saw Amy with a woman we knew to be a drug dealer. Payton squeezed my hand, trembling, her big green eyes tearing up.

"It should be you in that box!" she screamed at her mother.

That was enough to make Amy leave.

During the service, I didn't sit in the front row with the immediate family, but about halfway back, holding hands with my friends—Payton on one side, Sam on the other. Mom would always joke about arranging a marriage between Sam and me. She wouldn't be joking about that anymore, it dawned on me. The music played, and much to everyone's annoyance, the priest kept saying, "Christy was high, not on pills, but on life."

At the graveyard, the world was quiet as Mom's body was lowered into the pit. I watched Payton as she moved to the foot of the plot. Her hair was black and neon-green, and it flowed beautifully down her shoulders. She had her hands in her pockets, and she kind of squished her body smaller. A look passed over her face, her mouth caught between a smile and a heavy frown, her pierced eyebrows furrowed. A tear streamed down her cheek. I went to her, and we held hands.

■ ■ ■

I live in a clean, quiet house now. I love the people in it and its warmth. Something is always cooking, or playing on TV, or we're joking around. Aunt Jenny and her husband Ronnie have taken me in. No more screaming, crying, or smelly cigarette butts in the ashtray. I have a mother figure who reminds me of a mama bear, and a father figure who works like an ox, showing me that good men do in fact exist. I'm taken care of. Do I need a ride home? Would I like something to eat? I have the freedom to collect things, to add to my personal possessions, never having to worry about packing up to escape an angry landlord. I live with a cousin who is a grump, but he makes me smile non-stop. I have grandparents, religious and caring.

At times, though, I feel like I was plucked from my real family and woven into another, which is complicated. I've been separated from my siblings. Logan is off with an aunt and uncle. I haven't seen Brody and

A heartfelt memorial at the Portland McDonald's

Natalyn in almost a year. Last I heard, they were living with Timmy and their grandmother.

Sometimes I wonder if Mom's death was suicide. According to the autopsy, she'd eaten a Fentanyl patch—a pain killer that normally goes on your arm or thigh—and she'd ingested about twenty-four pills. She used to tell me that when she found the man she was supposed to spend her life with, my dead grandpa would send her another baby; she hadn't been able to get pregnant since Logan. After she started dating Timmy, it wasn't long until she was pregnant with a boy, and then a girl. She was convinced the pregnancies were a sign that she should stay with Timmy 'til the end.

As I type these words, it's been almost a year since she died, but it feels like weeks. I guess I tried to pick up the pieces and move on quickly; my instinct was to try to forget every detail of every painful memory. This probably prevented me from grieving fully. It must be hard for her friends to see me. I resemble her so closely with my whimsical style, pudgy face, and stocky build. I'm surprised people don't call after me with her name. Sometimes I worry that I *am* her, that no matter how much I try not to be a self-destructive person, it's my destiny.

Every day I'm conscious of avoiding her vices and making choices that will lead to a stable adult life. No drinking, no drugs. I plan to go to college but have decided against art school because I don't think it would earn me a steady living. I often fear for my friends when they take Xanax for menstrual cramps or headaches. I cringe when they take pills recreationally, saying "I just wanna feel good," or "I only take them every now and then," or "It's not a big deal."

I prefer to remember Mom when she was young. She has piercings, cool makeup, an irreverent T-shirt that says something like, "People like you are the reason people like me need medication." She has a big happy smile, her middle finger raised to all the bullsh-- in the world. That was Mom, my mom. And though I really miss her, I'm happier than I've been in a long, long time. ∎

SOMETIMES I WORRY THAT
I *AM* HER, THAT NO MATTER
HOW MUCH I TRY NOT TO BE A
SELF-DESTRUCTIVE PERSON,
IT'S MY DESTINY.

29

THOSE DAMN CHEAP TISSUES

Jason Fagan was one of my mom's best friends, as close as family. I've known him most of my life and never once has he turned me down or steered me away. I see him as a very important male figure in my life and love him very much. I interviewed him at his house, which is three blocks from my house in Portland. In his words, "This is my first interview without a lawyer present."

JASON FAGAN:

I would have to simply say your mom was my best friend. No one else was as close to me in that kind of way. She knew me inside and out. She knew my reactions before I knew my reactions. You just…you don't find that.

I met her at…not Angelo's…can't think of that other bar. I saw her a few times, and so I knew her tattoos and stuff. I was like, she looks pretty cool, man. We started talking and she was really down to earth. She liked Bobby, another good friend of mine at the time. They started hanging out and I was trying to hook them up and coach her in ways to get him. It was pretty cool.

PHOTO COURTESY OF CALLIE COMER

Best friends hanging out

Some of my favorite memories are the bonfires. Sitting out there drinking, playing music, watching the flames. No matter what I had in the fridge, Christy would drink it. Somebody once gave me this gallon of honeysuckle wine, homemade, and I tried it and I was like, "Oh, I'll leave it in the fridge. Somebody will drink it." Christy goes, "You got anything else in there?" I was like, "I got that wine." She was like, "I'll drink it." We always said we were going to have a bonfire in the dead of winter with snow on the ground but we never got around to it and that sucks. I'm going to have to do that for her and just sit out there, freeze my balls off.

Your mom put herself out before she would anyone else. Very compassionate, understanding. It was amazing. It blew my mind. I adored her for that, because in certain situations I'd only wish I could've been that way. She'd go without to help somebody else and that's for real. Or she'd go without just to make somebody else not feel uncomfortable. Whatever the situation was, she'd go that extra mile to make sure she wasn't stepping on anybody's toes.

She was very open. I don't think I'll ever meet another person as open as your mom and that's one of the things where we clicked so much because, hell, if you're going to have to lie about something you did you shouldn't be doing it. So we clicked on that, just open with all the sh-- we've done, the sh-- we do, the sh-- we're going to do. We were like that about everything, not just drugs or whatever. If we f---ed up we know we f---ed up. No point in lying about it.

Your mom was my memory. She'd start talking about a story and I wouldn't remember it at all. So she filled me in on all the sh-- I forgot. The sh-- I did when I was younger, she was right there with all the details, enough to kick it back in and make me remember. I really do miss that. I need that.

Methadone is trading one addiction for another. It's cheaper if you stick by the dosage that they give you, but nobody does. They're out buying that instead. And then they'll turn around and take their weekend doses and sell that and then turn around and buy it back. When Christy was on methadone, she was zoned, man. Not just on methadone, a lot of the stuff she was on. She'd just be sitting there in conversation and nod off. Her eyes would close and she'd kind of waver around a little bit, and then she'd come back and start talking like nothing ever happened.

And I'd tell her, "I can't stand it when you're like this. I just really can't." I told her a bunch of times. I guess life caught up with her. She'd been through so much with guys. She'd put her whole heart into a relationship and end up getting it broken. And then always having to find a place to live and move and then trying to find work. That sh-- weighs heavy on a person, and I guess she took pills as an escape. That's great as long as you can function, you got your bills taken care of, everything's taken care of.

Do what you want to do is the way I see it. But as far as it getting out of control, you got to step back and realize this is getting the best of me. You got to fix it.

I'd just say everything got to her, and hell, she just loved being high. When she died, I was just devastated, in disbelief, but at the same time, we all told her it was coming. I told her a hundred times. I always joked about it. I was, like, you're going to wake up dead. And f---, I wish she would've listened a little bit. Maybe a week before, she came over and hung out, and my vehicle was broke down or something and so we walked to the beer store. Oh man, she was just so messed up. She just kept falling behind. I had to stop and say, "Come on, girl, come on." She tried to sit down on the sidewalk, and that's when I knew she was pretty far gone. I tried to talk to her, but you know how she is. She thinks she knows her limits. I guess everybody does.

At the funeral, I was so tore up. Those damn cheap tissues they used were all over my face in little pieces from wiping my face so much. I didn't even realize. People started asking what was all over my face. F---ing tissue, man. For twenty minutes I'm trying to get it off, especially when they played "Jane." Man, that song. I just took bits and pieces of her life and added to it and wrote that song about her. And when you guys played it at her funeral it just…it got to me.

When your mom first heard the song, she was proud as hell. She was like, "Yeah!" And she deserved that. She'd been through hell and she's an inspiration to many, many people. Some of it she might've thought was a little worse than what it was, but some of it was pretty f---ing bad, and she'd get through it with a smile.

She'd been depressed about the whole situation with Timmy. She'd been with Timmy for God knows how many years, had two kids with him, and she loved him to death. And she started realizing he was cheating on her and he ended up leaving her and it devastated her. It really did. She came over here—I think it was for her birthday or something—and we had a little party or whatever. Just talking to her, you knew she was depressed, and all you could do was listen and give advice, or just listen sometimes.

What sucks is that she was really depressed at the end, but then she got you guys this new place to live and did a complete one-eighty. She called me and was like, "Jason, you've got to come check out our new house!" She was happy again. Then the next day she was gone. ◾

DAVID McCONICO

South 37th Street, Shawnee

The Man Who Mattered

From Cotter Homes to Shawnee

SOUTH 37TH STREET, SHAWNEE

In the morning the streets are exceedingly quiet, except for chirping birds and the occasional car passing on its way to work. You can go out on your porch, pull up a chair, and drink in the peaceful sunshine. But in the afternoon, things start to change. Everyone's up and out. From church events such as car washes, bake sales, fish fries, barbecue sales, and vacation bible school, people have things to look forward to. The parks get packed on Saturdays with neighborhood picnics and citywide events. There's always a reason to get out and stretch the old legs.

There's a strong sense of community here that comes from neighbors looking out for each other, or from just being neighborly—even the old-fashioned borrowing of sugar. It's not uncommon to hear someone say, "Hey, I cooked you a pie." The feeling of acceptance and family is set in deep in my neighborhood. My neighbors are young and old, tiny and tall, some friendly and some mysterious, others antisocial because they are protective of the peace on their street.

There is serenity and beauty in my neighbor-hood. The buildings, old and mysterious, are fine pieces of architectural craft with large columns that seem to extend into the past. The houses have an aura of home flowing around them from years back and years still to come. They come in a wide array of colors—brown, red, beige, blue. Each house looks different yet pretty alike—there is a uniform style. The businesses have friendly proprietors: Indi's, Marathon gas station, Shawnee Market, PNC Bank.

The serenity that I mentioned is sometimes disturbed by desperation. Someone might rob a store or a house. The police might start patrolling the block due to concerned neighbors. Or the blasting of an ambulance siren for an emergency that might be drug-related. People smoke weed and do harder drugs to try to escape. They shoot dice and gamble to make a quick buck in order to get high again. Their children are unattended, and the cycle continues.

Some of us hope to move out of the West End and make the money to do so. Others have the means to move elsewhere but are perfectly content. They appreciate the strong sense of community. Others can hardly make ends meet, which makes feelings like contentment and hope difficult to find. As for me, I just look for that golden band of sunshine that beams down each morning. It bathes me in its light, promising hope, change, love, and peace in a part of Louisville that has been neglected and misunderstood for too long. ▪

THE MAN WHO MATTERED

My grandfather was sitting in the passenger seat of his Lincoln Continental, waiting for me to start the engine and start driving. Funny thing was, I was a pudgy little ten-year-old boy. Excitement boiled in me. The car smelled of leather and sweet cherries coming off the air-freshener. I couldn't see over the steering wheel, so I raised the seat up. Then I buckled my seatbelt and made sure my feet could reach the pedals.

We were in the tiny town of Calcius, Alabama, in the driveway of my great uncle, Peter. His mobile home was faded white, and it had rust and cracks on its sides, making the thing look dingy. But inside, the place was homey.

Only a few minutes ago, I'd been bored to death, throwing rocks into the woods surrounding the property. My grandfather, mother, sister and I were down from Louisville for a "fun" family vacation. Most of my family who lived in this backwater strip of earth was elderly, and they didn't own any video games, or even a computer. The only entertainment in Calcius was playing with farm animals, or watching basic cable, or throwing rocks.

As I tossed what felt like my hundredth rock, the trailer door opened and Uncle Peter and my grandfather hobbled out chatting animatedly. "Boy, what are you doing?" asked Uncle Peter.

"Just tossing a couple of rocks," I replied lazily.

"Hey, there are plenty of fun things to do around here. Like cutting my grass," said Uncle Peter, barking up a laugh. "You can use my push mower since you can't drive the riding mower."

Uncle Peter was a bald man with little meat on his bones, and a walk that suggested hemorrhoids. He liked to jokingly pick on me. He'd tease me about sharing his brother's name—David McConico—or ask if I'd inherited his brother's terrible skills at the game of checkers. I enjoyed proving him wrong, and my grandfather enjoyed it, too.

"As much as I'd love to cut off your toes in the process of cutting your grass," I said, "I think I'll keep throwing rocks. And by the way, I bet I can drive that riding mower better than either of you two."

They both started laughing now. "If you're so sure of yourself," said Uncle Peter, "why don't you drive that old car of your granddad's there?"

"Now wait a minute, Pete," said Grandfather. "I don't want the boy wrecking my car. We'll be stuck down here."

"It's your decision, David, but the boy claim he can drive and I don't believe it for one minute."

Grandfather, smiling and shaking his head, reached into his pocket and tossed me the keys.

I looked at them in my cupped hands, not believing my eyes. "Are you sure about this?"

"Just get in the car," said Grandfather, going around to the passenger seat.

"Boy, oh boy," said Uncle Peter, "I can't wait to see this!"

I cranked up the engine, feeling like the luckiest kid alive. Then I rolled the window down and called out to my uncle: "Get ready to see a master at work!"

He laughed and shouted, "Try not to hit my trailer!"

Gently, I pushed the accelerator down, and the car eased forward like a great boat. At first, I couldn't believe this was really happening. I noticed everything: the trailer moving slowly by, the woods all around us, and the sound of the tires rolling over the gravel dirt drive. My grandfather was a cool customer, silent and poker-faced. I wondered what was running through his mind. Was he going to tell me to stop before the main road?

Uncle Peter with his wife and daughter

Portrait of the author as a young man

I made the decision myself, cutting the engine at the end of the driveway. I didn't trust myself to back up. I unbuckled, jumped out, and yelled, "Ha! I proved you wrong! I told you I could drive!"

Uncle Peter walked over and said, "Well, I guess the boy prove me wrong yet again."

Grandfather was wearing a proud smile. "He sure did."

It always made me happy to make Grandfather proud. He was my role model, a tall beefy man with hardly any neck, and salt 'n pepper hair. He had a confident authority about him, but not without a good sense of humor. We'd crack on each other about sharing the same name. He moved in with my family around the time I was born, and we did almost everything together. He taught me little life lessons, like how to polish dress shoes, how to wash a car properly, and how to tie a tie, though I still can't do that correctly.

He was also a selfless man who did things for others without asking for payment. One day we were walking in Cherokee Park, and a homeless man asked us for money to eat. Now, most folks would probably pass him by, thinking he'd use the money for drugs or alcohol. But my grandfather, who wasn't by any means wealthy, gave him five dollars. When I asked why, he told me, "I could tell from the way he looked that he really needed it. You never know what people might be going through."

■ ■ ■

If my grandfather played a major role in my upbringing, my biological father was the complete opposite. After seventeen years of my life, only a week ago did my mother receive her first child-support check from my dad. Guess how much it was? Exactly $13.50.

Until about two years ago, I used to forget my father's name. Maybe it was because I never met him, or the simple fact that my mother would talk about him only once out of every blue moon. I hardly ever wondered what he looked like. I strongly resemble my mother, so I rarely thought about what features I might have inherited from him. When I spared a thought in that direction, I pictured him as a dark-skinned, scrawny man, with a sheepish expression. I guess I pictured him sheepish because part of me wondered if he felt shame for not being a father to me.

On the rare occasion that I asked my mother about my father, it was the same question every time: "Mom, what's my dad's name again?"

She always gave me the same forgettable response: "Your daddy's name is Perry Mitchell."

Once, I asked, "Where's my father live?"

Laughing, she responded, "I don't know where he's at. I got rid of that man. Kicked him to the curb."

When I was little, most kids thought I'd be uncomfortable talking about my absent father. But I was the complete opposite; I'd be more than happy to tell them about my dad. I always gave them the same response: "My dad? Oh, I've never met him. And no, I've never bothered to ask why he's not around." Usually, I'd end this with a slight shrug and an unconcerned stare, and then they would drop the subject.

My sister, Tiarra, had a different father, who was absent also, but she used to talk to him on the phone when she was little. I'd wonder what it would be like to talk to my dad on the phone. I used to see all the TV dads on sitcoms and what a "normal" household should be like. At the time, I'd tell myself that a house with one parent and one grandparent was as good as a house with two parents. But no matter how hard a kid may try to act as if his or her life is normal without Dad around, the man is missing in action. His absence is like a dull ache. I never hated my dad for this, nor was I angry at my mother for not telling me more about him, but the love of my father was what I really wanted.

Life seemed to drag me left and right. I wasn't into academic success and never really saw the point in school, but I went anyway because I had the support of my mom and granddad. I did the absolute minimum to get A's and B's. I was a lazy smart person. All I ever wanted to do was sleep. I got made fun of at school because I was an overweight kid. I'd eat whatever was in the house, most of it unhealthy, and the pounds started adding up. If my dad had been around and working, maybe the added revenue would have allowed for healthier choices. My mother, who was overweight also, had no job and was on disability. Granddad didn't work. I had to be grateful for what I had.

It was spring of fifth grade when I was in art class trying my best to create a masterpiece, when a boy named James decided to pick on me. A pug-faced kid with short, unkempt brown hair, he liked to cause trouble. To James, I was an easy target.

"Move your backpack, fat-ass," he told me. "It's on my side of the table."

I kept working, not wanting to give him the attention he so desired.

"Dude, move your stuff before I move it for you."

"It's not even in your way," I said, still drawing. In my peripheral vision, I saw him ball up his fist, making the whites of his knuckles turn red. When he swung, I ducked and got out of my seat, staring at him. His expression was a mix of fury and embarrassment. When he swung again, I fired back, my fist connecting with his face just as his fist connected with my chest. We were fighting for a good minute before the young male art teacher ran over and pulled us apart. Out in the hallway, we were like wild wolves snapping at each other. The teacher asked, "Now what happened?"

I quickly explained my side of the story, and then James explained his side, claiming I started the fight, which made me even madder. I told the teacher he was lying, which of course made James madder, and

Me in my favorite red suit

then he swung and we were back fighting again. Our teacher got hit while he was trying to pull us apart, and then a security guard came running up the hall.

This didn't earn me the reputation of a tough guy and solve my problems of being picked on. The spectacle made me resent my classmates even more. I was ridiculed, put down, gossiped about, even by my so-called friend. To hide the shyness and pain I was enduring, I would be sarcastic, have a smart mouth. Somehow, I still made top grades. Whenever I got in trouble for talking back to a teacher, the punishment was light because I was a good student.

I didn't realize it at the time, but I was slowly sinking into a sea of depression. I was insecure and let things get to me too easily. I found truth in what people said about me. "Fat" and "ugly" were common insults in those days. I could never get up the nerve to ask out a girl. I would pray every night, and I'd always ask God: is something going to change? Am I always going to be this way? Please give me a sign if something's going to change.

Then something did change. My grandfather died. I awoke on a cold winter day, excited because today was my fifth grade Christmas party. I got dressed in a hurry and went to the living room. Grandfather lay on a bed in the dining-room, which was a temporary arrangement due to his illness. I passed by his perfectly-still body with a gleeful aura. I didn't think much of my mother's solemn expression as I watched for the bus out our front window. When the bus arrived, I bid my mother and sleeping grandfather farewell.

The day passed in a haze of food and holiday cheer. When school let out, it felt wonderful to be on Christmas vacation. When the bus pulled around the corner to stop at my home, I saw several cars parked in front of my house. They belonged to my aunts and uncles, and I felt a surge of joy. I thought a family Christmas gathering was taking place. I hopped off the bus, grinning from ear to ear.

As the bus pulled away, my uncle greeted me with a serious expression, and before I could even say hello, he flat-out told me: "Your grandfather's dead."

I walked into the house slowly, not bothering to greet my mother or aunts who sat conversing in the living-room. I dropped my stuff on my bedroom floor, feeling like a branch that was split from its tree. I felt guilty for passing my grandfather by that morning when he was deceased, and for

PHOTO COURTESY OF THE MCCONICO FAMILY

My grandfather in our house

having a pretty good day at school. I guess my mom just hadn't wanted to tell me. I cried more than I'd cried in years. My mother and one of my aunts came in to console me.

In my grief, I realized that Grandfather was my father when I didn't have one, a friend who always enjoyed my company, and a man whose values I wanted to carry with me 'til the day I die. For the first time in my life, I knew exactly who I wanted to be like. In the coming months, I started to think more clearly, and slowly things started to change for the better. No longer did I smart off to teachers, or at least not as much as before. I didn't let insults get me down as easily. I intensified my focus on school, and opened myself up a little more to class-mates, resulting in my three best friends, who to this very day understand me and have my back. Grandfather's death also helped me realize how short life is, and that I should value it more.

Me with my friend and Big Brother, Jeremy Rea

No one said life would be a nice easy spin down a driveway in sleepy Calcius, Alabama. You have to get out on the road and avoid accidents. You can't get too lost and wind up on the backroads of a broken life. I still have stuff I struggle with, like relating to girls and keeping my weight down, but I'm confident I can overcome those challenges and be a better person for having done so. I have a great mentor in the Big Brothers Big Sisters program, Jeremy, who has been taking me on college visits and helping with ACT prep. I just try to keep a positive attitude. If someone bothers me, rather than get angry or depressed I remind myself what Grandfather said that day in Cherokee Park: "You never know what people might be going through." ▪

NO ONE SAID LIFE WOULD BE A NICE EASY SPIN DOWN A DRIVEWAY IN SLEEPY CALCIUS, ALABAMA.

FROM COTTER HOMES TO SHAWNEE

This is from an interview I did with my sister, Tiarra McConico. Currently a student at Jefferson Community and Technical College, Tiarra is my best friend in a lot of ways, a kind-hearted person, even though she's a bit crazy and gets on my nerves sometimes. We talked about her views on our neighborhood, our family, and going to school.

Tiarra McConico:

I was born September 11, 1990, in Chicago, Illinois. Mom was in Chicago helping Aunt Katie with her newborn, LeAnthony, and she ended up having me. Mom was like, "Oh no, here you come! I guess I better go to the hospital." I was born at Bethany Hospital, the last baby the doctor delivered before he quit that job. I got the picture to prove it. LeAnthony and I like to say we're twins; we claim each other even though he's two weeks older than me. He's like a brother to me more than you are….no, just kidding.

I was three when I left Chicago and moved to Louisville. The first place we lived was Cotter Homes, by Park Duvalle School. That was my Head Start. A few years later, they

The McConico kids

decided to tear down Cotter Homes and we had to move again. They were going to build new houses, which became the houses that are there now. They were supposed to call people and tell them when they could move back but they never did. They just added new people. So yeah, we moved from Cotter Homes and never went back.

Since moving to Shawnee, the neighborhood has changed a bit, even though in my little world, it hasn't really changed. Like around me, there's different people moving in and out, a whole bunch of younger people, but as far as the community goes, everything seems alright and about the same. I consider myself to be very open-minded about my neighborhood and community. I've been robbed once, but I never let that bother me too much. I've never been shot at. When I lived in Cotter Homes, they always used to say it was the worst place, but we were never robbed there.

A couple of my friends, they love the West End. Of course, some want to move out, but most of my friends are split in half. Some don't really like it here, others do. Some seem to like it for a short period of time, but then they want to transition into something different or they've gotten into an argument with somebody and they just want to move away from it all. But still, everyone I know is pretty cool about living in the West End.

I like to do stuff to help out my community. I'm on the praise team at King Solomon Missionary Baptist Church. We're trying to build up our funds so we can help people out, especially the elderly. The praise team is called Judah Praise. We only started back in March, but we used to do other stuff through the church that impacted the community. We do what we can.

As far as family goes, it's been just Mom, me, and you—no father, of course. To me, life without a father…it's been good. That said, I don't know anything different. I'm sure things would be different with a father around. But I don't think it would be too different for me because I'm a mama's

girl. I call my cousins to find out what my father's up to and how he's doing, but I haven't talked to him in a while. I was twenty when I last spoke to him. We were at Uncle Leroy's church in Chicago, and my cousin gave me the phone, saying he wanted to talk to me. But he's never been involved in my life, not really, no. But I did find out that I have other brothers who have little babies. I have four older brothers in all, and I'm an auntie to seven. We talk on Facebook.

As far as my relationship with my little brother, it's just so terrible, he's such a…no, just kidding. He's pretty cool. I beat him all the time playing GameCube, though when it comes to Mario Kart he's the best and I will admit that. He always takes my sayings, he always takes my words. He's pretty cool, though.

Most of my time these days is taken up by school. I go to JCTC and I'm majoring in early childhood development because I want to be a teacher. I also work at a daycare, and I love going to work—most of the time. I love going to school, too, as long as it's not math class. It's a pretty good education system at JCTC. I learn new stuff and go different places, places I've never been, so school is a good way to get outside the community. My life is alright. ■

DEVANTE URBINA

North 38th Street

On the Grind

Fighting the Right Way

NORTH 38TH STREET, SHAWNEE

I missed the TARC bus to my job at McDonald's, and now I'm riding my brother's bike on a snowy day. I pass the abandoned garage on my street, which was once decorated with a red penis in spray paint. The bike is a BMX with a frame so small that my knees hit my chest as I peddle. I pass the house with the barking Doberman in the yard; I know that it's all bark and no bite, that I could jump the fence and remove the beast's collar if I wanted to.

I cross 38th to ride down Duncan—they're such bumpy, uneven streets. When the wind is right, I can smell delicious fried chicken being cooked at Indi's, and sometimes Chinese food across the street from my school. By the time I reach the 200 block of 35th, a stretch of abandoned houses I call "the abandoned block," I'm beginning to work up a sweat. It's hard to believe that such a desolate street leads all the way into Jewell Park, a nice place to hang out. Riding under the expressway, I'm honked at from behind for using the whole right lane to

Headlinerz Barber Shop

ride a BMX bike. There's a sidewalk, but melted snow runs down the wall and freezes on the pavement.

Heading down 34th, toward Kroger, I see the bigger houses perched on hills. Riding down Bank Street, I notice the alley that my brother and I take to get to CVS instead of walking all the way around the block. After 32nd, there is a viaduct for the trains; the columns of ice that form off this bridge can get as thick as a young tree. I pass PNC on 26th, where the clerks are extremely friendly, the same folks who worked at the bank when it was on the corner of Amy and Market, right next to my barbershop, Headlinerz. There's always an entertaining conversation at Headlinerz: sports, rumors, and the West End news. There is money to be made sweeping up hair, and sometimes, if you're short a few dollars, you can get a haircut on credit.

PHOTO BY DEVANTE URBINA

House in my neighborhood that I daydream about fixing up

As I pass LaPorte Park, I slow down just a bit, thinking about all the memories. Parks in the West End have played a big role in my teenage life. There was LaPorte, where I sat and had a long conversation with a potential girlfriend, who told me about the platforms in the park where drunks hang out in summertime. Lannon's Park was the place to smoke cigarettes, play basketball, and pick up the dirt bike trails that run by the river. Jewell Park is so secluded that I could visit with a certain girl with extremely protective parents, so we could sit on the bleacher and talk about her dreams of going to the University of Kentucky and my uncertainty about how life will work itself out. Portland Park I remember for a long day spent with my ex-girlfriend, after getting blizzards at Dairy Queen. Shawnee Park was where I ruined a pair of Jordan I's by sprinting up a muddy hill.

Almost to McDonald's, I see the tail end of the bus that I missed. I really wish I were riding it and not my brother's bike. The TARC is a breeding ground for entertaining conversation—strangers actually talk to each other in the West End. The buses are always crowded because a lot of people don't own cars. There are usually people waiting at every stop, and conversation revolves around money, how little of it one can make doing odd jobs, and how much the government takes in taxes, and the Louisville Cardinals. I watch handicapped people board the TARC and receive smiles. When the elderly get on, youngsters sacrifice their seats. Out the windows there are plenty of uplifting sights. I once witnessed a couple of teenage boys take a snow shovel from an elderly woman's hand and finish shoveling and salting her sidewalk.

My quads are burning as I pull into the parking lot of my second home, the Portland McDonald's. When I moved to the West End from my neighborhood in Toledo, I was amused by the negative reputations of Shawnee and Portland. I was told how rough my new home would be. If only more people were aware of the teenage boys I witnessed take a snow shovel from an elderly woman's hand. ◼

Bus stop where I sometimes write

ON THE GRIND

Sitting on the asphalt, hands locked behind my back, my head is throbbing. The headlights of the patrol car are shining directly into my eyes. I'm fourteen and returning to juvenile detention in Toledo, Ohio, back to the white block walls and florescent lights too bright to sleep under. The police have slashed my bicycle tires and slammed me to the ground. My forearm is turned outward, making my gang tattoo well visible: a Mexican gangster in a fedora and sunglasses, a.k.a. the "pachuco face."

"If you're not hiding anything," says the blue shirt and badge, "why'd you run?"

"Instinct," I reply.

"Yeah, right asshole. Where'd you throw it?"

"Throw what?"

"The gun, the drugs, whatever it is you're hiding."

"I'm not hiding anything, Officer."

"Sure you're not. You live three houses down from this alley. You expect me to believe you're not hiding anything when you ran this way? Why didn't you run to your house?"

My gang tattoo, which I got when I was fourteen

PHOTO BY DEVANTE URBINA

"It was instinct."

"Nice shirt. Woodward High School Football, huh?"

"Yep."

He nudges me in the back with the flashlight, wanting me to fess up, to confirm his suspicion that I've broken the law. He's right to be suspicious. My sleeveless shirt reveals other tattoos, and my baby-blue bandana is folded and tied around my head. I'm out on the streets at 4:00 a.m. without any shoes on, but the cop merely laughs at my sock-feet, not thinking to interrogate me about where my shoes went. I'm certain he doesn't know that I stole the bike, unless the owner reported my description—highly unlikely.

This isn't something I'm proud to write about. But it's part of my history and a story I need to tell. My homies and I chased the kid in our Lincoln Towne Car. "Hey, where'd you get that bike?" I shouted from the back seat. Jay-J was driving, Ricky was in the front passenger seat. The poor kid peddled as fast as he could but must have realized that he couldn't last longer than the gas in the Lincoln. He stopped after four blocks, in front of a church. Nothing he could do but face us in front of the church.

I got out of the Lincoln while the other guys held tight. "Where'd you get that bike?" I demanded.

Fearing for his life, not only did he tell me where he obtained the bike, he gave me the exact address of the guy he bought it from.

"Take me to him. You can ride the bike, I'll get on the pegs." This was a bluff; I planned to punch him off the bike.

"Here, just take the bike, man."

"What?" I shouted, and threw my first punch, knocking him off his feet, and attempted to connect again before he hit the ground. Then I punched him while he was covering his face, my adrenaline pumping so hard that I slipped out of my sandals and didn't realize it. Then I stood back and let him struggle to his feet. "Run!" I shouted, and off he went. I waved to my homies so they knew it was okay to leave, then grabbed the bike and peddled off, leaving my sandals in the grass.

It was common practice when stealing a guy's bike to ask where he got it, because you could claim that it was yours, that the bike was stolen from you, which gave you the right to steal it back. I attacked the kid just to show my friends that I wasn't scared to hurt someone. I had to be intimidating to keep their respect. I was on the grind, trying to survive on the streets any way I could.

The patrol car, a lonesome pair of headlights on an empty street, spotted me when I was almost home. Instead of playing it cool, I rode back the way I came. Even though the cops never figured out what I was hiding, it didn't matter. I was headed back to juvie for breaking curfew.

■ ■ ■

It's cold and the wind is snapping at me. The trees are screaming, "Hurry up!" I'm walking as fast as I can without looking suspicious. If I walked any faster, I'd be running. The night has fallen upon me. If I don't make it home by 10:30, I'll lose something that I've experienced just this once: an extended curfew.

My probation officer didn't allow this, my foster mother did. I'm being trusted. I'm supposed to be responsible, level-headed.

I have a new beginning in Louisville's West End, where my life is calmer. The Shawnee neighborhood seems like a tranquil paradise compared to my neighborhood in Toledo. If you'd known me only eighteen months ago, you wouldn't believe I am the person I am today, a senior with a 4.0 GPA last trimester and a 27 on the ACT. If you'd opened your ears to me, you'd have only heard what the streets of Toledo had to say, and the streets didn't know me. Nobody knew me. People knew my name, and they knew my face. Even when I wasn't incarcerated, I was still a prisoner. A prisoner to poverty in a city that Forbes.com ranked #8 in their 2012 list of "America's Most Miserable Cities."

I've been to juvie for assault, fighting in school, curfew, and underage consumption of alcohol. I was also arrested for possession of a dangerous ordinance, because I thought it'd be cool to make a Molotov cocktail—my mother knew it was time to report my dangerous tendencies, and called the cops before I had a chance to use the explosive. I believed that drug trafficking was going to be my way out, rather than working a backbreaking blue-collar job that wouldn't even feed my family. I believed that the only battles in my life would be between gangs in the South End and the East Side of Toledo.

I'm the oldest of four brothers and a sister, from four different fathers. There's Larry, now sixteen, Victor who is fourteen, Juan who is eight, and there's my sister Hadassah, six. All of my siblings have faced obstacles of poverty, physical abuse, and mental issues. The adults in our lives have faced their own challenges: drug addiction, molestation, alcoholism. I came to believe that a single-mother household was the best situation for children, because men were destructive forces.

For several years we lived in public housing, an apartment in the projects. We rented a few houses that we couldn't afford for long—the landlords were ruthless, never understanding or helpful enough to let us pay rent even a week late. Our clothes, which were mostly stolen or handed down, smelled of mildew because we had a washer but no dryer. Mom had a job, yes, and at one point a boyfriend helped support us financially, but it was never enough, and the emotional distress was terrible.

I felt Mom's negativity every time I made an entrance into the kitchen. "Stay out of my fridge, fat-ass," she'd say. I was overweight and she regularly crushed my self-esteem. I rebelled against her every time she tried to impose her will on me. She was fierce in attitude, mostly stubborn. Men found her appealing, a 5'2" redhead who gave birth to me at the age of fourteen. Larry came two years later. Early in our childhood, she wasn't as callous. She'd make food packages for the homeless. We once brought a homeless man into our house during a blizzard. He was at the bus station with no socks. We fed him molé chicken. We let him take a shower and sleep in the living room. I admired my mother.

Our father, Henry Urbina, worked in the grain elevators for Anderson's Grain and Ethanol, and drove a gleaming blue Mustang with racing tires. He died when I was two years old, and along came Nicho, who was a decent dad to us at first. He spoiled Larry and me, calling us his Little Protégés, and even took us to work with him. While he was scraping shingles off roofs we'd be piling them into the back of a pickup truck. Nicho bought us treats and took us on family trips to Texas. We even had nice birthdays and Christmases. Then Victor was born, and along came the most ridiculous "house rules" ever. We were beaten for things like leaving the shower doors open. Extension cords, coat hangers, belts, and other household items became devices of abuse. The man was broad-shouldered and stocky, like a Hispanic pitbull. He was never a bad guy in our eyes, but he seemed very temperamental, and he had his favorite: Victor.

At the age of thirteen, I decided to become a boy who didn't call a single place home. I couldn't take the verbal and physical abuse anymore, and took to the streets, sleeping from couch to couch. Every acquaintance became a best friend, out of necessity. The mother of one friend treated me like family, letting me take showers, and even bought me Christmas presents. When she found a nicer house to rent, I helped them move in, but after a week she told me I had to leave. Her daughter was pregnant and it'd be too much to take care of both a houseguest and a newborn baby. I guess it was true. She knew the elements that she was putting me up against. In the cold winters of Northwest Ohio, there isn't much time to find a place to sleep before your body gets numb and your nose begins to run.

My sleeping situation became very complex. I slept on the cold concrete of a friend's garage, under a picnic table on a rainy night, and once, in the back of my mother's minivan. For the seven months I was on the streets, my mom never attempted to look for me. I never called. She once drove past me without even honking the horn.

Because we were close in age and shared the same father, Larry was my closest family member, and still is. We'd sneak away together to catch up. We'd talk about how the Dallas Cowboys were doing, or Larry's developing talent for street fighting, or the dogs at our house—pretty much anything I was missing out on. We'd talk for hours, eating nachos from the gas station. Larry was never a fan of chili on nachos, but he loved the cheese. We made jokes on each other about how our bodies were develop-ing—Larry liked to make fun of my short legs. I cracked on him because he didn't like rap music. We'd talk about girls. The whole time I'd be dreading our separation. I knew that once I walked Larry home, we'd shake hands, give each other a manly hug, and then I'd have to turn my attention to finding a place to sleep that night.

Though I kept going to school, drinking and drugs became an issue. Four Lokos—a caffeinated malt beverage that's like cocaine in a can—stole my sanity. I'd stumble and

fall on my face, a thirteen year-old unable to speak coherently enough to ask for help up. I took ecstasy in school one day; my best friend and I split a blue star and a blue dolphin, and I stayed wide awake for two days. There were shrooms, too. Once while I was tripping, my friend told me not to look in the mirror because I'd see evil spirits, but I did anyway. My pupils were so dilated that I couldn't tell the color of my eyes. I smacked myself in the face and it was totally numb. I wanted the trip to stop and tried to eat it off, an entire bag of pepperoni, and then I noticed blood dripping from my mouth onto my shirt. My cheeks were bleeding from the inside because I hadn't stopped chewing. Then I ran to all my friends' houses in the neighborhood, banging on doors. They didn't answer.

Another night, an older friend of mine invited two women over. He was eighteen, the women were twenty-one and twenty-four, and I was fourteen and willing to try anything. My friend told me to "en-tertain" the twenty four year-old so he could enjoy some time with her friend. I wasn't attracted to this woman, but because my friend was allowing me to stay in his house, I felt that I had no choice. I didn't know what to do, exactly, so I had to ask him. "Tell her that you want to hit it, and hard," he said.

I told her, and next thing I knew she was pulling me to the floor with her tongue in my mouth. Her breath stunk of alcohol and, unless I was mistaken, sautéed onions. I was completely grossed out and feeling taken advantage of, but somehow I got excited. She realized it, and instantly jammed her hand down my pants. She seemed very experienced; she unclothed me in less than a minute. I didn't know where the time went, or my virginity.

■ ■ ■

My mom left Victor's father; she finally got fed up with his abuse. But the next man in her life, the father of my little brother Juan, Big Juan, was affiliated with a Mexican drug cartel. He drank a lot and was a powerful figure physically, wide-shouldered. His skin was dark brown, his features Aztec. His curly black hair was always greased, his gold necklace always gleaming.

Larry and I would spend time at the drug house starting around the time I was in fifth grade. It stood out from every other house in the neighborhood because it was well-maintained, even had a white picket fence. There were Ford Expeditions and pickup trucks with chrome rims. The living

room television was a huge flat screen with a console that held a DVD player, a VCR, and a stereo receiver that connected to speakers throughout the house. There was an expensive carpet in the front room, an eggshell-white color that contrasted nicely with the hardwood floors. No children were allowed in there.

It would be easy to think the men who occupied this house were hardworking immigrant laborers, always fixing the place up. They didn't dress too fancy and had regular day-laborer jobs. They were mechanics, always wrenching on cars. But if you were to ask the owners of the local businesses about these guys, they might give you a different description. Not only did these men import drugs into the neighborhood, they imposed their own kind of order and law, which wasn't necessarily a bad thing. Whenever there was a fight or some type of commotion at a neighborhood business, all that was necessary to restore order was for one of these men to show his face.

We young boys were spoiled by the cartel, not only Larry, Juanito, Victor and me, but every male child in the "family." There were dirt bikes, ATVs, videogames, new clothes and sneakers. The only time I ever saw anyone sit in the front room was when the men in suits came over. At ten years old, I didn't understand that they were high ranking bosses from Mexico, but they seemed very special for some reason. They never parked on the street or in the garage, but in the back yard on the grass, so they didn't have as far to walk into the house with whatever their suitcases contained. Also, their cars were expensive and very suspicious because they were imports; nobody in the North End drove foreign cars unless they dealt drugs. The fence had to be opened and the above-ground pool taken down, so they could park. They wore zoot suits, baggier than traditional suits, and hats with wide brims and gold chains with pedants, the Virgin de Guadalupe. Their mustaches were pencil-thin, well-groomed.

Larry and I walked in the dining room one day to find stacks of hundred-dollar bills covering a banquet table that stretched long enough to fit fourteen people. I'd seen it filled with people, but never cash. I'd known Big Juan and his buddies had lots of money, but not this much. Most of it probably belonged to the men in the suits, but a good chunk of it stayed. Piles of cash had been in many dreams of mine. My friends and I had played the hypothetical game "What would you do if you had a million dollars?"

There had to be at least a half-million on the table. I had no idea that it was drug money. Larry and I approached, cautiously, and started touching it, just to see if it was real, or a mirage. Then we heard loud conversations in Spanish coming our way.

"Come on Larry, we have to go," I said, tugging his shirt.

"Can I take one? Please?"

"With all this money, I bet we could take a few," I whispered. "But no way."

The men entered seconds after we exited through a different door. I couldn't stop thinking about all that cash, and we reentered the room a few minutes later. The men in suits had no problem with our presence, but Juan's dad seemed nervous about it, like our presence would upset his bosses. But one of the suits gave my shoulder a squeeze, and another rubbed Larry's head. Maybe they saw us as potential employees.

Big Juan was the only man in the house who didn't hold a regular job. He wasn't as smart as the other guys. He blew his money on attention-grabbing items, like a Chevy S-10 with chrome rims and a loud block-beating stereo system. He was the one most likely to be followed by the FBI. He'd go to a place called Club Mystique and rent out pool tables all night. Instead of buying shots, he'd buy whole bottles. The stupidest thing he ever did was stash heroin in the engine of his truck and go on a drug run with my half-brother Little Juan, who was only an infant. Heroin expands when heated. The plastic wrapper exploded and the engine seized up, causing him to crash into a telephone pole. My brother wasn't hurt, but the police came and arrested Big Juan, who was then deported.

■ ■ ■

The father of my sister Hadassah was out the door quicker than the first trimester of my mother's pregnancy. I just know that he was Lebanese, a Christian. After he left, another man claimed to be Hadassah's father, and still to this day, he'll insist that Hadassah is his daughter. We call him Tiger. Everybody in the neighborhood called him Tiger. Larry and I liked him as soon as he started coming around, beginning when I was about twelve. We could relate to him. He was from Jordan and didn't look fully white, black, or Hispanic—just like us. He didn't like the police and told us that he was a rebel in his home country. He once rolled flaming gas-soaked tires down a hill at police cars. His stories excited us.

Working in a corner store as a clerk in our hood, he learned about gang life and drug activity, crackheads and the street prices for guns. He made fast friends with gang members, the same men I admired just because they had money. Tiger was making lots of money too, but not so he could buy chrome rims and party. He started selling crack and carrying guns so he could feed my family.

Riding around with Tiger was like riding around with a celebrity. It was unusual for drug dealers to let some Arab guy stroll into their trap house, but Tiger was famous and even had keys to the houses. One afternoon, we visited six houses, and Tiger left each one with either weed, or money, or a new kind of gun that I had never seen before.

Even though he was trying to be on a grind as a gangster, Tiger stayed loyal to his religion. He was a follower of Islam and would wash and pray multiple times a day. He never threatened to hit us, loved our mom, supported us financially, and claimed us as his children. Once he'd made his way into my mother's life, he never left. He was in and out of my life only because I was in and out of my home by choice. He made jokes at my expense plenty of times, but I didn't mind. "Man, when I first came around you were shaped like a basketball," he'd say.

"Man, I think I could take you," I told him once.

"Dude, I am grown man," he said with his Arabic accent.

"Come on, let's try."

"No Devante, I don't want to hurt you."

I grabbed his head and tried to put him in a headlock, but with lightning speed he pushed my elbow up, locked his arms around my chest, picked me up and threw me on the couch. Then he began play-punching me in the stomach. I knew the damage could've been pretty bad.

Though I was only a teenager, Tiger viewed me as a man. He told me that it was very common for a man to start his life young in the Middle East. Even though I was running in and out of the house all night long, not for good reasons, he never said anything judgmental. We smoked together sometimes, a blunt or two. He didn't care if I got drunk. The police were my enemy, he told me, because they would try to stop a man's hustle by any means. He believed that the criminal justice system is corrupt, and that society forces you into bad situations. Poverty forces you to break the law in order to survive, and the justice system already has a punishment prepared for your reaction to being poor.

But he didn't believe that crime was the only way out. He made me focus on my education. "Man, do what you want, but if you don't stay in school I will not f--- with you. I will not help you anymore." And so I stayed in school. He let me work with him in the store to make extra money, but it wasn't much. I wanted to make friends with all the drug dealers that ran in and out of there. I wanted to be known. I wanted to be as popular as Tiger was in the hood.

Then one day things went wrong. Two guys tried to rob the store at gunpoint. I wasn't there. One guy had a TEC-9 semi-automatic assault gun, and Tiger shot him dead with the store's .45 caliber pistol as he was emptying out the lottery register. The second dude had just locked an elderly customer in the restroom and was running down the aisle with his gun raised. Tiger shot at him, chased him outside, and then shot at him some more as he was running down the street. When Tiger returned to the store, he locked the door behind him, forgetting about the customer locked in the restroom. He shot the dying robber twenty-six more times using the TEC-9.

The police interrogated Tiger and then released him, saying that he couldn't

My stepdad Tiger, in Jordan

return home. They watched the house that night for the fugitive robber, one known for killing and revenge; it was possible he'd come to the house to kill Tiger for killing his buddy. After catching him somewhere else in the north end, they arrested Tiger because he was no longer useful. He was being charged with voluntary manslaughter.

Tiger called home every other day, standing in the phone line in jail for hours. He spoke to every member of the family, telling us that he loved us so much. He said it so sincerely. He apologized for shooting the man so many times, but the guy had held a TEC-9 to his head and he feared for the sake of his family. I attributed the twenty-six shots to adrenaline, not hatred. He wasn't trying to prove his manliness. He was that scared.

Though he was found not guilty, Tiger was deported about four months after he was released from jail. He was pulled over for speeding, and not only did he lack a driver's license, he was still involved in a case with the INS that had been ongoing since we met him. The time for the judge's decision was near. He'd immigrated to the U.S. to further his education and had a school visa, but within the first year he dropped out, fearing that after he graduated he'd get sent back to Jordan. Though he always spoke to me about finishing my education, he didn't practice what he preached. He now says that he couldn't afford good lawyers for his immigration case. He told us that his lawyers would make racist comments and act as if they were joking.

Tiger's absence caused a whole new struggle in my family. It left my sister without a father and my brothers without a male role model. But we still keep in touch via email, Facebook, and Skype. Even though he's far away, we still love Tiger.

■ ■ ■

The streets began to wear on me. By the time I was fifteen, I was sick and tired of trying to find a place to sleep every night. It was hard not knowing when I'd get a decent meal. I wore borrowed clothes or clothes that I had to steal. I wore shoes that weren't mine. I was always insecure because I knew that the person who owned what I was wearing could take it back; anything I needed for basic survival could be snatched away. I wanted to move back home very badly, but didn't. I was determined to show my mother that I could find success in my life without her help.

I found a new home. My homie Ricky had a sister named Josie who was in her twenties. One day after a party, we started talking about my living situation. She said that if I really wanted help that her mother, Andrea, would be willing to take me in. I had met Andrea before; she was like the "Hood Mom." She fed all the kids in the neighborhood whenever she cooked a big meal and coordinated the neighborhood football team. She was also a drug and alcohol counselor.

"'Vante, this is serious," she told me. "This is a commitment. If you really want to live under my roof, you have to get on the right track in school and you have to follow my rules."

"I'm really tired," I told her. "I look like I'm aging already. I want help."

"Then you'll be going to school every day. In by 10:00 on school nights, 11:00 on weekends. If you ever need a ride, call me. I'd much rather you call and let me know you're stranded than leave me guessing where you are."

"I understand."

I felt deeply grateful for this opportunity, and still do. Andrea talked to my mother, and they came to a custody agreement. I was going into Andrea's temporary custody. At fifteen, "temporary custody" meant until I was eighteen or ready to go back home, but I didn't think I'd ever want to live with my mom again. There was a woman willing to take care of me. Andrea had an unspoken agreement between the assistant principal, Mr. Slusser: whenever I got written up or upset, Mr. Slusser was to call Andrea immediately. Whenever I spoke to her, her voice calmed me down. Andrea could tell me to shut up, even, and I'd listen and continue my day peacefully.

I began to feel like I was capable of doing things besides surviving on the streets. I could pursue any career I desired. Andrea encouraged me to participate in sports, chase intellectual development. Woodward had plenty of enrichment programs, sports, and adult leaders. Mr. Slusser got me into the SAAB program, the Student African-American Brotherhood, which helped me develop leadership qualities. In that program I was introduced to drug dealers who had been shot and stabbed but who had turned their lives around, had even attended college.

They wanted to tell their stories to help kids like me. I realized I still had a chance to be successful, even though the odds weren't in my favor. At the first SAAB meeting I attended, Mr. Slusser spoke to the members: "Last year someone asked me, 'You're white, so what can you tell me about being black?' My response was that I'm not here to teach you about being black. I'm here to teach you about being a man.'"

Andrea advised that I stay in the SAAB program as long as possible, and I stuck with it until the day my mother called to say that Larry had been arrested. He was being charged with second-degree assault. The severity of that charge varies from state to state—in Ohio it was a charge that could be easily dropped—but the family had recently moved to Kentucky. Even though Larry was released quickly pending his court date, my stomach turned inside out. Now that I was doing so well, I could see that Larry was headed down the wrong path. I felt that I could've prevented Larry's situation had I been around to help.

I told Andrea that I wanted to go help my siblings, and that I didn't care what opportunities I would miss out on. My siblings lacked good financial support and structure in their lives. To my surprise, Andrea supported my decision. She thought I'd grown up enough to make my own life choices. On December 7, 2012, I boarded a Greyhound for Louisville, oblivious to how complicated my life would become.

As soon as I arrived, my mother informed me that she would be leaving for Jordan to visit Tiger. She left in three days and wouldn't return until mid-January. Our aunt, Mary, was supposed to stay with us at my mom's mobile home. But Mary went back and forth to her house, and one day, while she was gone, the police came to pick up Larry. No matter how much I pleaded, I knew they wouldn't let him out of those handcuffs.

"Sheriff, what did he do?" I cried.

"It's just a bench warrant. He has court tomorrow."

"He doesn't have court tomorrow."

"He does now."

I assumed that Larry was headed to juvie to start serving time. His assault case had already been settled in court; he'd been found guilty and was awaiting his sentence. But this wasn't why Larry was being taken away. The landlord of the trailers had reported him as an abandoned child. The landlord didn't think much of my mom's parenting.

I called my aunt and told her what had happened and that I'd stay the night in the mobile home; she could pick me up in the morning. I didn't want her to drive over in the dark. But come morning, it wasn't my aunt who showed up but the sheriff, who said he was taking me to court for Larry, so my brother wouldn't be alone. Except the sheriff was lying. I was put in a holding cell at the courthouse and waited all day for someone to come talk to me. I didn't receive anything to eat. I broke out in a cold sweat. Finally, at the end of the day, I was brought before the judge; she hadn't known that I was being held, let alone why. Larry's probation officer explained the situation from her point of view: I was an abandoned child, just like my brother. The judge declined to rule on that, but said that I be held for a few weeks because I had no representation by a lawyer or a guardian.

That night, I rode with Larry and one of his co-defendants in the assault case in a squad car from Louisville to Elizabethtown. Handcuffed and not allowed to talk, we were headed to Lincoln Village, a regional detention center for youth. Our mother knew what was going on—my aunt had called her—but she couldn't rush home because she couldn't afford to change her flight or purchase a new ticket. She wouldn't return for another five weeks.

Lincoln Village reminded me of a library, ironically enough, because it looked so nice and modern from the outside, and there were many cars parked in front, like patrons. I watched as the guards aggressively patted down my brother and then led him off to his unit. His intake had already been processed because he was there the night before. As I went through the intake process, I looked over at a board with a list of bunk assignments. There were no empty slots, not a single empty room.

In the open area of the unit were two tables with four connected stools on either side. Four plastic chairs that resembled small recliners were meant for inmates with higher privileges. The cell doors were painted green, and fluorescent lighting shone brightly through the small windows. The place smelled sterile, like a hospital.

I was forced to sleep on a cot in a cell already occupied by two guys. My brother was confined on the other side of the building. I was worried that an overcrowded jail riot would unleash itself at any moment. I lay on my cot looking up at my cellmates sleeping on the bunks, trying to size them up. In the morning, I realized my cellmates

were two scrawny guys in the lower five-foot margin. I wasn't worried about protecting myself from them, and soon enough, after going to a few meals and getting a feel for the place, I wasn't afraid of anyone. I could handle myself against any kid in the facility. Eventually some inmates were released, and I was moved to another unit. My new cellmate was named Gillespie—inmates went by last name only. The guy was hilarious. He always had an amusing sex story or a comical rap song to share at night, the only time we were allowed to talk. He made lewd gestures behind the backs of the guards.

I learned how to gain as much freedom as possible at Lincoln Village, which I thought of as stolen freedom. Because we weren't supposed to talk to our cellmates, I learned when the guards would come around so I could talk more. I could hear them tugging on the doors, making sure they were secure. Sometimes, you could catch them while they were off doing laundry and get into a deep conversation. You could also listen in on their radio conversations. One night, as they were checking my door, I heard "Larry Urbina in transit from 610-bottom to 310-top." I was in cell 410 on the top bunk and knew that Larry's new bunk was directly adjacent to mine.

"Larry, it's me," I said through a crack in the wall. "I love you."

"I love you too," he responded.

This exchange happened every night. Every night, we told teach other that we love each other. Even though he was just on the other side of my wall, I felt as if I had abandoned him. I felt like I'd completely failed my purpose of keeping him out of trouble. All of the progress I'd made for myself in Toledo was gone. I had no idea what the judge would decide about me when I returned to court. I didn't have any criminal charges in Kentucky, but my record in Ohio worried me a ton, even though all my cases had been settled.

I never saw Larry during the day because inmates on different units were kept separate—some guys were co-defendants. At meals we weren't allowed to raise our gaze from our trays unless in conversation with a guard. It was maddening to know that Larry might be across the room but that I couldn't look. Then I figured out a strategy. When the automated locks to the chow hall clicked open, it was loud. I'd hear it, wait a few seconds so the entire line of inmates could file in, distracting the guards, and then I'd try to sneak a look at my brother.

I turned seventeen in jail and spent Christmas in jail. On Christmas Eve, all units were moved to the gym, and we played volleyball and cornhole. I was put on a team with Larry only once. The entire time I bragged on his athletic ability and reminded him of our memories from playing in the streets as a child. All the while, we kept up our intimidating appearance. It wasn't Larry's first visit, so people already knew his violent reputation. Therefore, they knew mine as well. But I wanted to show my brother some type of affection because we would be separating soon. You couldn't turn your head without seeing a guard with his eyes on you, and it was against the rules to touch another inmate. I just gave him a high-five and wished him a Merry Christmas, and then we returned to our units to change clothes and cool off for the meal. Christmas dinner consisted of turkey, gravy, dressing, mashed potatoes, cranberry sauce, and a brownie that was topped with peanut-butter-fudge icing twice as thick as the brownie itself. You almost felt as if you weren't even incarcerated. You could talk to people in your unit quietly. Larry was in a different unit, so I had to make eye contact from across the cafeteria and smile.

On New Year's Eve, I had no way of knowing when the clock struck midnight, because after bedtime at 8:00, we had no way of keeping time. I only knew that I'd be starting 2013 in a green jumpsuit. I was sickened to be spending the holidays in jail, but I was even more hurt that my little brother was doing the same thing. I would've chosen to suffer twice as much if it meant Larry didn't have to suffer with me.

I wanted to kill myself. I thought about it so much, even considered ways that I could do it fast, before the guards or my cellmate could stop me. I tried to convince myself that there was enough water in my cell toilet to drown myself, but I knew there wasn't.

I prayed on New Year's Eve, and woke up in the morning realizing that if I committed suicide I'd truly be abandoning my family. I also realized that I was too scared of God to kill myself. Growing up, I was told there were only two ways to be barred from heaven: not believing that God was the Father, and suicide. The way hell was described—a fiery pit that never stops burning with scarred souls screeching at all hours—didn't sound like a fun place to spend eternity.

I cried over my life, thinking about all the poor choices I'd made, how the circumstances surrounding my life had been less

than ideal. And after I'd cried myself to exhaustion, I realized I couldn't change the circumstances of my past. I couldn't change that I had no father, was raised in poverty, was abused, or that I had wasted a good chunk of time in detention centers. But I could change now. The damage was still fixable. I started to think about the possibilities that still existed for my life. I was still only seventeen, and I could make changes before I turned eighteen. If I wanted to be a man, I knew what it took. A man would help anyone humble enough to ask, would care for his family, would claim his responsibility.

We took academic classes at Lincoln Village, and I tried to be the first "student" to have the right answer to every question. I began reading about the fluctuating, hormonal teenaged mind, and read a book on how Christians deal with teen issues, though I wasn't religious.

Larry and I returned to court in mid-January. It wasn't a courtroom but more like a conference room, with everyone seated around a long table. The judge sat at the end like the Godfather. Larry's probation officer, early forties, had blonde hair and garish, red lipstick. I knew that she was going to say negative things about my mother and our family. She commented on how my mother couldn't control Larry, and how she couldn't provide us with the basic necessities for survival. By this time my mother was back from Jordan, and we were hopeful that we would be leaving with her that day. But the judge ruled that we be held in detention until they found us a foster home. It wasn't the first time my mother watched her boys escorted from a courtroom in handcuffs, but it was the first time she watched us leave together. This time she had the guilt in her eyes, not us. I still wonder what her thoughts were, if she wondered how our lives were in jail.

In early February, a social worker named Jamie came to pick us up at Lincoln Village. Man, was I happy to see her. She was tall and extremely attractive, like a model, and I noticed the guards puffing out their chests.

"I'm taking you guys to the west end of Louisville," she said in an ominous tone.

"What does that mean?" I asked.

"There's trouble to be found there," chuckled one of the guards.

"We'll be fine," I said.

"It can be a rough place," said Jamie.

"We're some rough kids," I said, feeling like I needed to sound tough.

"I can vouch for them on that one," said the guard.

Driving to Louisville, I promised myself

not to squander the opportunity that was coming our way. I was going to look after Larry. We'd do everything we could to ingratiate ourselves to our new foster parents.

"These people are older," said Jamie, "and they just want to help. Don't try to take advantage of them."

That stung. She said it as if she really knew Larry and me, as if we were both criminals. We were going to the Batten family, Muncie and Barb, an older black couple in the Shawnee area of Louisville. As we walked into their house, a social worker from Boy's Haven, the foster care agency, said, "The Battens love to cook."

"Well, we love to eat," I responded cheerfully.

Everybody laughed. Muncie was wearing a University of Kentucky hat, and he made lots of jokes. Barb made small giggles here and there. I knew we were in a great place. By the grace of God, Larry and I had landed in a safety net.

■ ■ ■

Sometimes I'll go lie down in Larry's bed while he's watching television. "Come on, man," he'll groan, "you got your own room." Meanwhile he's scooting over to make more space for me. I feel so blessed that there's

With Larry at our homecoming game

no longer a jailhouse wall separating the two of us, that we live in such a nurturing environment. Larry's thankful too, though he's more reserved in how he shows it. We both go to The Academy @ Shawnee, only a few blocks away. Larry is my teammate in football, wrestling, and track. I spend all my time with Larry, other than the time I spend working at McDonald's.

People around Shawnee know about our past; we don't hide anything. Our football coach jokes that we should become lawyers, because we spend so much time in court. Larry says he wants to be a paralegal. He likes messing around with the law. He takes interest in why laws were passed and why they were ever proposed in the first place. Our next trip to court will be a custody hearing for Larry. I'm eighteen and have already recommitted to State's custody. Larry isn't old enough to make that choice yet, but it would be great for him to stay in Shawnee. He calls it home. It's a place where he can focus on school, participate in ROTC, and be with his girlfriend.

Every time I went to jail in Toledo, I hoped that I could just stay, because I thought life was easier in there. I didn't have to worry about bills, an education, women, children, or where I would be sleeping at night. Now I like to go outside when it snows, because I'm no longer fighting the cold at night. I appreciate that I'm able to use the restroom whenever I need to. I have access to food when I'm hungry. At school, I'm president of Men of Quality, a program that instills leadership qualities in young men from all walks of life.

There was so much to fear on the streets. My only fear as of now feels more like a luxury: that I won't be accepted into my dream school, Vanderbilt. But I'm confident that I can be successful at whichever college I end up attending; I'll take advantage of every opportunity, and then I'll go on to even greater things. During my first incarceration at a detention center, I told a guard that one day I was going to write a book. I jumped at every opportunity to clean the floors, toilets, showers and tables so that I could earn commissary. I used it to buy a journal and would write small essays about my experiences. Maybe, one day, I'll write that book. I'm on the grind in the best way possible. ■

PHOTO BY ALAN MILLER / KERTIS CREATIVE

EVERY TIME I WENT TO JAIL IN
TOLEDO, I HOPED THAT I COULD
JUST STAY, BECAUSE I THOUGHT
LIFE WAS EASIER IN THERE.

FIGHTING THE RIGHT WAY

There was always the fear of losing myself, but the one person I was even more scared of losing was my brother, Larry Urbina. To some people he's the distant type. If that seems to be the case, odds are he's in deep thought. The sixteen-year-old kid with the hair of a soldier, 5'7" and a muscular build, will never make it in the military where his first dreams stand, but despite the wreckage from the first broken dream he continues to pave a boulevard to his fame and fortune.

Larry Urbina:

As a kid in Toledo, I was bullied for years because I was small, skinny, and couldn't even do one pushup. Between ages seven and about twelve or thirteen I was being attacked every day—on the way to school, in school, after school, and sometimes even at home. So I had no choice but to learn to fight, and I fought a lot.

We were rough kids, even when we were having fun. I remember rock dodgeball, where we'd throw rocks at each other and I'd try to show off because I was on the dodge-ball team at school.

We would hop on trains and ride them around the city. We also did things we shouldn't have. We usually had to work to pay for our own clothes, but we would also steal from people. I remember once we beat up this kid and took his shoes. I took many things over the years. I've taken clothes and stupid things like headphones and other things I really didn't need but wanted.

When we moved to Kentucky, we lived out in the country. I learned more positive ways of helping the family, like helping to cook, clean, and watch the kids. But I still had a lot of aggression and I got into several fights. I ended up in juvenile detention pretty much the whole summer of 2012, and then again from December 2012 until about February 2013, when you were there with me.

Detention was hard. I missed things from normal life that I didn't think about until I was there, like nature. Just looking outside and smelling that grass. You really want to touch it while you're in the back of that car travelling about two hours back to court. Detention helps a lot with your patience. It actually it helped me a lot with my reading, too, got me into reading a lot. I enjoyed some of the fiction they had. My cellmate became a close friend, and he taught me a lot about what I could have done for myself to avoid the mistakes he had made. He was older, seventeen.

When we were in detention together, you and I weren't actually allowed to talk. We couldn't see each other because we were in different units. But it turned out that our cells were connected to each other on different units and there was a huge crack in the walls so you and I could talk to each other every night. Every night, at the beginning and end of our conversation, we said we love each other.

We always did basic exercises to stay in shape, and we did other ones to show off a little bit. We did basic pushups and pyramids. Pyramids are harder than basic pushups; you hold the pushup while counting down in your head. I showed you how to do one-handed pushups and Superman pushups, when you lie on your stomach and push your whole body up with just your arms. And then I tried to show off by putting my feet up on the concrete bench, and doing pushups with just one hand.

One of the guards taught us how to do a lot of workouts. I remember one of the guards, Mr. Williams, tried to give us a life-lesson every day. Unlike most of the other guards, he actually cared about us and tried to talk to us. He asked us what we cared about.

The court said it was looking for a family for me and you. We didn't get the news that we were leaving until about maybe two weeks before we actually left. They told us that we were moving to the West End of Louisville. Everybody said it was a horrible place and there were gang members and people being attacked and a whole bunch of stuff. But once I got to Shawnee, it seemed like what I'd expect out in the hills where the rich people live. There were no prostitutes, no people fighting. I expected gang members to be standing on the street loitering, but I saw none.

Mom's friends still talked bad about the neighborhood and thought we were bad because we were living in the West End. They had a fear that we were going to be shot or killed or something crazy like that, because they look at these people who have tattoos and all this other stuff—how people look on the outside—and don't think about how they are on the inside. That's how some people look at you and me.

Being in a foster home was kind of hard first because I had the fear of not knowing anybody in the neighborhood, and getting to know everybody in the household was a worry too. Our foster parents tried to help us out as much as possible, and they still do. We can go to them with anything that we really need. A lot of good things have happened since I've lived with them. In school I've gone from low C's to A's and honors classes. I try hard in school because I know I really want to succeed. I have a lot more time to focus on my school work and try to actually make something better of myself. I also play football and I wrestle.

I would've liked to join the military after high school but can't because I have a heart problem—I wouldn't pass the army physical. But I know how to be a soldier. In everyday life it seems like being a soldier is just doing what you do. Like what our coaches say, sacrifice and discipline, committing yourself to something that you need to do and want to do and doing it the right way. I'm trying to do things the right way now, and it feels really good. ■

Devante Urbina

93

JODECI THOMAS

SOUTH LONGWORTH AVENUE, SHAWNEE

ETYMOLOGY AND ANODYNES

NEVER USED AN ALARM CLOCK

SOUTH LONGWORTH AVENUE, SHAWNEE

I grew up on a street called Longworth, at the very end of Market Street. "Murder Market" is what they call it. There wasn't any murdering on my block, though. There were two parts to Longworth, and one end was nicer than the other. I lived on the rather rough side. It was a nice street, but things did happen—normal things to us—like neighbors fighting with one another, and house and car robberies every now and then. Then there were the not-so-normal things, like drug busts and riots in the middle of the street. But we all saw each other as family and helped each other out on Longworth.

It was me, my mother, and my little sister Angel living in house 105 on the south side of Longworth. I remember our neighbors well. There was Mr. Charles, who lived in the green house and was very good friends with my parents. He always brought me and my younger sister Angel little gifts, like a candy bar or a bag of Grippo's, the chips that were both sweet and a little too spicy for a six year old. We loved Grippo's from Mr. Charles.

There were the Mitchells, two of whom were my age. Jaylyn Mitchell had caramel skin and long black silky hair, somewhat like a foreigner would have. We played together a lot when we were young, until she stole my bike. Then there was her sister, April. All I remember about her is the day we were playing hide and seek. She was having trouble keeping up with me, and I called her fat. I was nine or ten years old, and I knew what I was saying, but I didn't care. Sometimes I look back and wonder what would have happened if I hadn't done that. She pushed me down and ran home and cried, and after that day we weren't friends again. What a bad experience I had with those Mitchells.

There was Ms.Rita, who always had a Bud Light in her hand and was always yelling at someone for the littlest things, like running in and out of the house too much. One Halloween we went to her house—I was Cheetah Girl and Angel was a clown—and Ms.Rita accidentally spilled beer in the bowl of candy. My sister and I ended up eating beer-covered Reece's. But Ms. Rita really loved us, and always made sure that if we needed anything, she would be there.

There was the old lady with a "toy poodle" that probably could have eaten me alive; she had a granddaughter who came over—I think her name was Carmen. She only came out and played when her grandmother let her. She was very nice. She shared her popsicles and played tag with us. Then there was the lady with the big yellow house, who had two poodles, one white and one black. Everything about her house was yellow, even the decorations in her yard, including the fancy lawn chairs and the bird fountain.

There was Derrick, who moved to Longworth when I was about twelve. He had pretty hazel brown eyes, really bushy eyebrows, and a really nice smile. When he first moved to Longworth, he didn't talk much, isolated himself from the rest of us. Once he got to know us, he got more comfortable, and now he's like family, always hanging out with us and joking around.

Jodeci Thomas

There was Lashonda, who lived across the street. She loved to dance and had a passion for doing hair. I knew her because her mom was in charge of the dance team I used to be on but got kicked off of for never wanting to practice.

There was Day Day and Corn, short for Cornelius. They were brothers, but looked nothing alike. Corn was the oldest and I knew him the best, only because we went to middle school together. He had dark skin, like me, and pearly white teeth. He got in many fights at school and confrontations with his teachers. Day Day was just young and silly, the type of kid you just had to bear with. They lived with Ms. Sheila, their aunt. I loved her because she always told me stories I shouldn't have heard at the age of eleven, like all of the crazy things she did at the daycare she worked at when her boss made her mad, and confrontations between her and some of the kids' parents. She loved animals, had three kittens, two dogs, a rabbit, and even a turtle that Cornelius found in their backyard one day.

Then there was Isaiah, who lived around the corner from everyone else. I met him in first grade. He used to be so little; his head was always bigger than his body. He liked to laugh and goof around with everyone.

Even though I live on a different street now, eight blocks away, Longworth will always be home.

ETYMOLOGY AND ANODYNES

In my neighborhood, it isn't cool to go to school and make straight A's. They'll make fun of you and call you "lame." You don't get props for making perfect attendance and honors around here. Maybe from the older people, but not many in my age group appreciate things like that. The kids just want to know what hood you represent. Do you like red or do you like blue? Red means you're a Blood and blue means you're a Crip. They want to know how many times you've been to jail, or if you like to smoke weed. I guess I'll be lame. I don't smoke or drink. Coming up in a household where alcohol was an escape from reality, I decided to do otherwise.

I get this mindset from my father. He was my biggest motivator and my number one fan. No matter what I did, he was always rooting for me and always on my side. He had a way of making me feel like the smartest dumbest kid around. When I did dumb things growing up, he always made me feel like I did nothing wrong and whoever said it was wrong was an idiot. Saved me from a lot of whoopings from my mom. He would always try to hide me from her or make her laugh so she would forget about what I did. Don't get me wrong, my mother and father loved each other; he just wasn't going to let anyone lay a finger on his baby girl. My dad would literally go to war with the world over any of his children.

He was a tall caramel man with dark brown eyes, and bald as could be. Sometimes we made jokes about him, because he didn't have any hair. I would call him "baldy" or "scallywag." He would always respond with a nose joke, like "big nose girl" or he would say my nose was bigger than my face. Of course, I take after my father. He passed the big nose and teeth right to me. I take the dimples from my mother.

My dad loved my ambition and he always taught me new things. When I told him I wanted to be a lawyer, he was so proud. He would throw out big words like "etymology" or "anodynes" and tell me the definition. He would say, "If you're going to be a lawyer, you need to know this." I would grab a notebook and get to writing. I carried this dream of one day being a lawyer on up into high school.

He always encouraged me to be myself. When I was little I used to dress up for dinner all the time. I would switch out of my clothes into something fancy like a Cinderella dress, and I even went as far as wearing my little heels and tiara. My dad never called me weird when I did this; he admired me for it. Even if it meant walking around pretending to live in a castle, he would go along with it.

My dad also supported another passion of mine as a kid: dancing. At every family event when I heard one of my favorite songs I would start dancing. Some of my family members would call me "Jo Jo Dancing." Embarrassing, I know. Something about dancing kept my body energized and I liked it. It made me feel free. I tried out for all the local dance teams, like Young Diamonds and Souljettes, and usually made them. My dad loved that I found something that made me so happy. He loved the fact that I was very competitive, too. In middle school, when I tried out for the dance team he bought me an outfit for each of the four days of tryouts. When I didn't make the team, he was angry at the coach because he knew that was something I was good at. He knew that when I really cared about something I went for it, no matter what.

Something else that helped me develop the confidence to be my own person growing up was the Shawnee Boys and Girls Club. To this day, it is a second home to me. I've been going there since I was nine.

Playing dress-up as a kid

My mother wanted us to go somewhere so we wouldn't always be home alone when she was at work. She thought my Dad was a bad babysitter, because he was always asleep and gave us whatever we wanted. He would take us bike riding and feed us candy for dinner. My cousin Jessica told my mother about the Boys and Girls Club.

At first, I was shy and didn't go to the Boys and Girls Club too often. But the people there were very friendly; they asked if I wanted to join in little games. They shared food with me, helped with my homework that I brought from school, and if I was upset they wanted to know why. The people I met at the Boys and Girls Club really grew to by my friends. They became family to me, because they cared about me so much.

When I turned ten, I ran around the club telling everybody that I was happy to be in double digits. In three or four more years, I could go in the teen room. Anybody that grew up there knew what that felt like. At the Boys and Girls Club there was an art room, a dance room, a computer lab, and a big gym. You had to be thirteen to enter the teen room, though, and when you get old enough to go in you start to feel like you're running things. The staff members let you do more, and when you get in trouble they

don't make you sit on the bench by the front doors for a punishment. You go on better field trips.

Sometimes going to the Boys and Girls Club made me forget all the bad things in my life, like arguments with my mom or that big test at school that was coming up. They took us on field trips everywhere. Sometimes they were educational, like UPS, and other times they were just to have fun, like Holiday World. I learned a lot of things about life and about myself through the Boys and Girls Club. They taught me skills that I needed to get my first job, at Indi's—how to dress appropriately, how to carry myself, and how to be prepared with a resume. I even learned how to run my own little business. I painted nails at the Boys and Girls Club for a dollar. I had my own employees, too. I would give them twenty-five percent of my earnings at the end of the week and make them brownies as a reward. They even let me have my own room to run my nail salon. I sold candy bars at school, too. I always found ways to make a quick hustle.

Mr. Rob was the head man and most of the kids there were afraid of him, because he was always raising his voice and he had a really rough look in the face. He was a tall,

The Boys and Girls Club where I have spent so much time

very cut forty-five-year-old man. He had a full beard and a big smile. He was brown, a little shade lighter than my little sister. I never figured out why, but he loved my sister and me. We were little trouble makers, but he always let us slide. I guess it was because we were so willing to help around the club with the other kids, like serving lunch and watching the younger kids, so they wouldn't kill each other over games.

Ready for my first day of fourth grade

Another person in my childhood that shaped me into the person I am was my first love, Josh, also known as Rell. Josh is short for Joshua, and Rell is short for Tyrell, his middle name. I don't really remember how Joshua and I met, but I do remember how our romance started. Josh had a complexion a little lighter than mine, light brown eyes, a perfectly round face, and a wide smile. He had really wavy hair that he described as being "Cherokee Indian hair." He lived in the very last house on my block, about five houses down.

One day, we were playing hide and seek, and we tricked my little sister and told her to go hide, then ran to his house and hid on his porch. I was scared that his grandmother would come outside, and he held my hand for comfort. Then he asked me if I had a boyfriend. Since I was five, the answer was no, but I did have a crush on a kid at my daycare named Little Joe. Josh asked if I wanted him to be my boyfriend. I laughed, and he went on and on about how he was strong and how he could beat all the boys up in our neighborhood if they messed with me.

From that day on, I guess I had the hots for him. Until one day in second grade when we got in a fist fight at school. He was trying to egg on a fight between me and some other girl. He pushed me and told me to fight her. Then I turned around and punched him instead of her. He grabbed my arm and it turned into a cat fight, with us rolling from the auditorium stairs into the lobby and rustling back and forth with each other, and that didn't end very well. I'll never forget that day. When I got home, I had scratches all over my face, and the majority of them carried on to my neck. To this day, he still has the scars where I scraped his face. Mine were gone the day after, because my mom covered me in cocoa butter that night.

My mother told him he couldn't come over anymore, but he came to apologize to me a couple days after and said he wouldn't do it again. Then we were together again. I loved him and he loved me, the whole shindig. He wasn't afraid to be that different kid in the crowd on the block. He did weird things like collecting caterpillars and carrying them in a jar to show everyone. He found them in our neighbor's backyards, and sometimes he would just walk up and down the street searching for them. He found a rainbow wig in my closet and would wear it around the neighborhood. People would make fun of him and even call him "gay" or a "fag." I think we were around eleven when he did this. I would just laugh, because he didn't care what other people said about him. He did anything to make me laugh or call him "stupid." He used to get me to go for a ride on the back of his bike, and we would go sit at "the beach" along the riverside near Shawnee Golf Course.

We would talk about some of the things that made us mad, our futures, things that made us laugh, and all the tons of crazy things that went on in our households. He would tell me about silly things like how he got in trouble for getting smart with his teacher at school and how his grandfather whooped his butt. I would tell him how I locked Angel in the bathroom for snitching on me. And we used to talk about creating a future together. He used to say we were going to have twenty-one kids and live in a thirty-room mansion.

We were a couple on and off all the way up into high school, when I realized there were other boys besides Joshua on planet Earth. Before then, he was all I really cared about. I didn't want to know anybody else. But I guess people just grow out of things. We change as we get older and develop different interests. I feel like the passing of my father had a lot to do with that.

I was thirteen years old when my father passed, and it was the beginning of my eighth grade year. It was day after he took my sister and me to the Kentucky State Fair, September, 1, 2009. At his funeral, you could tell how much of an impact he had on people's lives. People who I had never even seen before came to pay their respects. So many people came that there wasn't enough room for everyone to have a seat—we were literally hip to hip. A lot of people loved my father. Something about his spirit touched people. He always knew how to make a person feel good when they really needed it, with his warm embrace, big smile, and loud and everlasting laugh.

After he passed away, I guess I just stopped wanting to do things because he was gone. I didn't want to be bothered with people. I started to isolate myself. I didn't like being around anyone or anything that reminded me of him. Not because I wanted to forget him, but because it upset me to think of him. I wanted to put the thought in the back of my brain. The way Joshua cared for me reminded me of my dad, so I avoided him. I also stopped going to the Boys and Girls Club.

I still wanted to be a lawyer, though, because that's what I told my dad I wanted to do. He always made sure I had what I wanted, and now this was something I would have to do for myself. If I really wanted to be a lawyer, I had to work hard for it, but it seemed like no matter how hard I tried, I kept getting behind in school. I had trouble staying focused, and I almost failed eighth grade, and then I almost failed ninth grade, and finally in my sophomore year at Male High School, things caught up with me.

I had seen Male, a school outside my community that had a really good reputation, as a way to get out of this hole that people in my community are put in. Now that I had to leave Male, I was headed for a school with the worst reputation of all, The Academy @ Shawnee. People said there was no hope for that school. They said the kids who go to that school aren't smart, and all they do there is fight. Scared and unsure, I couldn't do anything about it. I just had to deal with the problem I created.

My first day at Shawnee, I prayed that the thirty-six weeks of my junior year would fly by. I prayed that after it was over, I could return to Male. The faculty at Shawnee were very blunt with me. They told me what I needed to do to get where I wanted to go,

PHOTO COURTESY OF THE THOMAS FAMILY

My father holding me when I was tiny

how I needed to bring up my GPA and how my test scores weren't very good. They actually sat me down and showed me that they cared. They made sure I understood everything that I was being taught. Shawnee made sure its students were first priority.

It was rocky in the beginning. People called me "bougie" and "stuck up" because I came from Male, but little did they know I lived right down the street in Shawnee. After a few altercations and a couple of one-on-one activities at school, they started to see me as a person, not just "the new kid." Dr. Hawkins, my English teacher, was the first real friend I made at Shawnee. I always loved English, but I really looked forward to seeing that woman every day. She was a fair-sized white lady with long blonde almost-gray hair. She wore big reading glasses and always painted her nails gray. She had a beautiful smile and eyes that would never lie to you. I always felt better after talking to her. She saw the potential that I had and made me feel special. She would be upset with me when I didn't do things to the best of my ability. She knew I wanted better for myself and my future. She always pulled me to the side and complimented me on my work, and offered lunch at McDonald's, and sometimes I would sneak out of class just to go see her before she left the building.

Now I'm sitting here in the middle of my senior year. Now that some more time has passed since my father's passing, I've become a little more involved with Boys and Girls Club, and Josh still remains an important person in my life. We still have our good talks and goofy moments, and he still goes around being weird. I've been accepted to both Northern Kentucky University and University of Louisville, and I'm waiting to hear from other schools. I'm grateful for all I've been through, and I'm excited to begin a new chapter in my life. ◼

MY DAD LOVED MY AMBITION AND HE ALWAYS TAUGHT ME NEW THINGS. WHEN I TOLD HIM I WANTED TO BE A LAWYER, HE WAS SO PROUD.

NEVER USED AN ALARM CLOCK

Darlene Thomas is my mother. She is fifty-two years old and could tell you many stories about life, because she's seen it all. She is a very important piece of my life. She may not always be the kindest or most understanding human in the world, but she makes sure I never go without. You are only blessed with one mother, and one only. All is love.

DARLENE THOMAS:

I grew up in the Russell neighborhood. My mother originally was born in Mississippi. We lived at 1710 Magazine until I finished elementary school. Then we moved to 18th and Chestnut, and I went to middle school, went to Manly, then Noe Middle. I was one of the first students in Noe Middle when they first built it. And from there, I went to Parkland for the ninth grade. That's the year that they started busing. And from 10th to the 12th grade, I went to Ballard High School, where I graduated in 1979.

In high school, I had a lot of friends. Got good grades. Perfect attendance. No doubt. Because Momma made sure you went to school. You went to school and you went to church. That was just one of her requirements. When Fridays came, all the other kids were so happy, but we weren't. Because we still had to get up early on Saturday morning, clean up, go to choir practice, get up Sunday morning at 8:00 and be at church at 9:00 for Sunday school. Then church started at 11:00, and went all the way to 2:00. So, there was really little time during the weekend. That's why I still get up so early now. That's why I don't use an alarm clock to get up. I've been at my job twenty-seven years. Never used an alarm clock.

I can't remember the little community college that I went to, because they tore it down and renamed it something else over and over. It was off of Crums Lane. Went there for the medical assistant program. Got my degree in a year. But I didn't go right into the medical field, because every time I see a needle, I hyperventilate. Instead, I worked at a hamburger stand on 34th and Broadway. I can't remember the name of it. It's a liquor store now. It didn't go too well, because I knew they were selling food that didn't taste right. And every time I said something, the owner told me it was my taste buds, but it was the nasty food. He was a real prejudiced man. He didn't want to hire white people. I didn't like that. I'm not that kind of person. He told me scrub around the base of the wall and get on my knees, and I'm not going to do that for anyone. So I just told him, "You tell your mother to get down there and get on her knees, and you have a nice day." Turned in my uniform to get my last check, and left. Never looked back.

After that, I went and worked at a hotel called Roy Inn. It was on Dixie Highway, across the street from Bojangles, over by the old Dillard's. I stayed there for five or six years, but I knew there was something better in life than cleaning somebody's rooms. So I went back and got a degree in interior decorating.

Well, I still wanted to do nursing, so a friend of mine asked me to come out to her job at a nursing home, and I was just playing around, filled out an application, and they hired me right there on the spot. I've been there ever since. It's been four different names, but now it's called Camelot. Been there for twenty-seven years. I like taking care of old people. I really don't know why. I just do. They have so many interesting stories they can tell you about life. I never liked hanging around people my age anyway. Even when I was younger, I hung with older people, my aunties and stuff.

■ ■ ■

As a girl, when I got out of school I would always go and get everybody's newspaper on the block. I was not allowed to go in anyone's house. My aunt told me, you know, things can happen, and one particular time, one man told me that he was too sick to give me the money, to come in the house. I said, "I can't come in the house." And he kept insisting he was sick, so I went in and got the money, and I left, and I came back – gave everybody their paper – I made him the last one. Back then, some people had their living room as their bedroom. When I went back, he had moved off the side of the bed to a chair. And I said, "You told me you were sick. I can't come way over in your house." And he said, "I barely made it over here. Can you just please hand me the paper over here?" And I kept saying, "I'm not supposed to," and dummy me, I went around to the chair where he was. I handed him the paper, and he pulled the cover off of him. He had no clothes. I ran out of the house so fast. I was so scared.

I ran past my uncle, and he came in the house and asked me what was wrong. I couldn't even talk. They gave me water and everything. When I could talk, and I told him what happened, he said, "You stay right here. I told you don't go in nobody's house." Well, he went down there, snatched the man out of the house, and oh my goodness, beat him unmercifully. Good Lord, he whooped him. Then he came back and he whooped me for not doing what he told me to do. I learned from that. He wasn't playing with me. Not at all. That's the uncle I can never forget. His name is Jewell Thomas. He was my father's brother. He was more like a father than an uncle, because he did so much for us. My mother had five kids, but we didn't need for anything. He didn't have any children, so he considered us his children.

■ ■ ■

I met your father when I was sixteen. I met him up there on Beecher Terrace at the community center, Baxter Gym. I think it's between 11th and 12th Street, off of Muhammad Ali. I remember when I met him. We were going to fight. He was bothering me. He just kept talking to me, and I didn't want to be talking. That's been so long, I don't remember all of what he was saying. I pushed him. I didn't see him any more for a while.

PHOTOS COURTESY OF THE THOMAS FAMILY

Our family

He came over to the house one day with my older brother Carl Lee, and I said, "That's the guy I was telling you about." And then, you know, that's how I met him. He just started calling me. I started dating your father when I was seventeen. My mama didn't like it. She really didn't want us talking to anyone in the neighborhood. She just wanted us to be the best we could. She didn't like having anybody over to the house, none of that. She didn't think your father was a bad person, she just didn't want him around. He was a good person. He didn't do anything to anybody. Everybody was crazy about him. He just had one of those personalities. ▪

NALA WINEMILLER

South 40th Street, Shawnee

The Perfect Break

Mud Puddles

SOUTH 40TH STREET, SHAWNEE

I live in a neighborhood near the Shawnee football stadium, quiet when football season is over, kind of like a graveyard, the grass dead but the soil full of history, the sweat and tears of games won and lost.

I live in a neighborhood that is rich with people who strive against hardship and help each other out as much as they can, even when they are not related by blood.

I live in a neighborhood where old houses stand tall, the antique homes watching over the neighborhood as it changes into something new and less unique than before.

I live in a neighborhood where people show off their tattoos proudly. The ink embedded in the skin is a badge of identity that gets flashed often.

I live in a neighborhood where the neck of the small woods is the perfect place to become whatever or whoever you want to become, for however long you want or need to escape.

I live in a neighborhood where the park is brand new, an unpolished and uncut gem, waiting to show everyone its shine.

I live in a neighborhood where it's normal to have cracks in the sidewalk, on the side of your house, in the windshield of your car—cracks that show something has been through hell, but they are seen as warrior scars and not a disgrace.

I live in a neighborhood where the dark night is the quietest part of the day. The deep bass of the passing cars remind you that you aren't alone, that there are other people outside your locked door.

I live in a neighborhood with giant old trees that are prettiest in fall, the leaves red, yellow and orange, floating down to the streets, making them beautiful.

I live in a neighborhood where negativity is louder than positivity and carries the farthest, while positivity only carries to the end of the street.

I live in a neighborhood that is for the most part a place of peaceful silence, the wind gliding over the smooth day and night, nothing loud or rude puncturing the air. ▪

THE PERFECT BREAK

Bold, bright light breaks through the fog in my head, pulling me into a white room…a bathroom. Why am I in a bathroom? How did I get in here? I press my hands against the sink, fighting a wave of dizziness, and look up at the mirror. Slowly, very slowly, the face of a sixteen-year-old girl comes into focus. The right side of her face—pale skin with freckles, a full dark eyebrow, an unfocussed hazel eye, a petite chin—is undamaged.

But the left side, oh my God: open wounds on the forehead and cheek, skin of the upper lip and chin absent, a blue bruise in the corner of the eye closest to the nose, reminding me of someone who applied eye shadow in the wrong place.

Who is this girl? What happened to her?

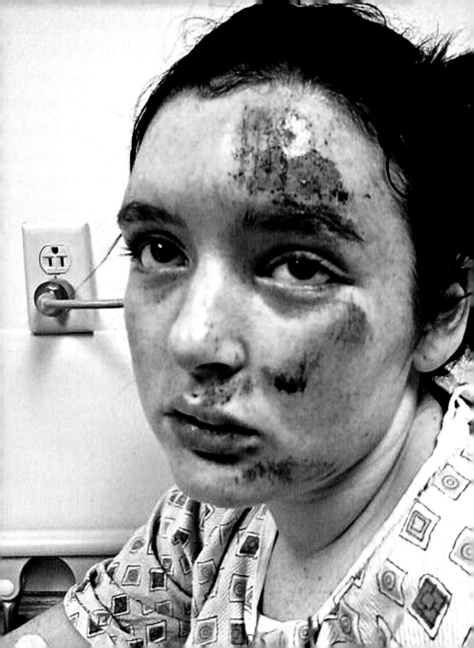

I stagger out of the bathroom, into a hospital room. My mom is seated in a chair next to the bed, her coppery hair curled under her chin. She looks exhausted, as if she stayed awake by my side the entire night. Like recalling a strange dream, I remember that I asked her to take a picture of my face, just minutes ago, because it hurt so badly. And that I threw up chili into the silver tray-bowl thingy.

Who convinced me to eat chili? My mother? I always hated chili, the beans seeming to be nowhere and everywhere at the same time.

"What happened to me?" I ask.

She inhales and exhales, as if she already told me several times. "You were at your friend's house and it had snowed…*a lot*." She looks down at her feet, as if it's hard to talk about. "You guys went over to the church to sled. Apparently people had four-wheelers and were driving around in the snow."

I have no recollection of four-wheelers, and I tell her so.

"Well, some guy tied a car hood to a four-wheeler. He was pulling people around on it. You didn't want to go, but they bullied you into it. They peer-pressured you into it, and they were spinning around when the rope broke. You hit a telephone pole face first."

I stare at her, trying to remember if this is true. I feel lost. She explains that the other kids riding on the hood rolled off before impact. Somebody shouted, "Bail!" Did I know what "bail" meant? No, she didn't think so. She says that rather than roll off, I turned my head away just before I hit the pole. The doctor thinks that turning my head saved my life. But my skull took a terrible blow, and I'm suffering from memory loss.

Suddenly I remember that when I was in the bathroom looking in the mirror, my hair was straight, not curled. Why can't I remember who straightened my normally curly black hair? Wait, black hair? My natural color is red, just like my mother's hair. Why is it black?

Mom tells me she dyed it a month ago. A feeling of panic drills through me. How could I have forgotten something I had wanted so badly? It had taken me a year to convince her to dye my hair black. Then I realize I can't remember what day or month it is, or even the year. And what's my name?

I don't ask my mother these horrifying questions. I don't want her to panic. Later, when the doctor comes to tell us about the x-rays, I learn that I broke the entire left

PHOTO COURTESY OF THE WINEMILLER FAMILY

Me shortly before the accident

side of my face and both eye sockets. He says that I broke the bones "perfectly," meaning none of the little pieces fell out of place, like a web of cracked safety glass. I wouldn't have to have reconstructive surgery, but my face was as fragile as a potato chip. There was a chance that I could regain my memory, and a chance that I would never get it back again. It might improve, or get worse. For the time being, I had to avoid any movement that could jar my head and send all the perfect pieces into my brain.

■ ■ ■

Me shortly after the accident

My mom was mad about the four-wheeler. She thought it was such a stupid accident, the result of parents letting their kids behave recklessly. An adult who had been present had called my mother to say she was taking me to the hospital, but Mom had insisted on picking me up and taking me herself. I was discharged after two days, and my face started to scab over after a week, my black eye turning an ugly yellowish color that looked like stomach bile. Gross. Following doctor's orders, I didn't play rough, eat hard candy, play my trumpet, or walk "flat-foot," meaning I had to walk on my tippy toes. Worst of all, I wasn't allowed to laugh. Laughing could kill me.

I moved gingerly all the time, whether it was making Kool-Aid or letting the dogs out in the yard or sitting down on the couch. I'd get scared whenever someone reminded me of an event that took place only a week ago. How could I not remember the pep rally when surely I sat through the whole thing? I repeated jokes to friends and family. My favorite was to say that when I hit the telephone pole I must've wanted to call someone. Or, I'd say that someone was trying to call me. After everyone stopped laughing, I'd repeat the same joke, having forgotten that I just said it. My back hurt a lot, along with my head. I had to shift positions in the car because a slow pulse of pain would spread through my lower back. The light was too bright for me even when the clouds waded over the sun, so I had to wear sunglasses.

When I was allowed back in school, two weeks after the accident, I had to walk carefully around the hordes of jostling middle schoolers in the hall. They seemed like deadly weapons. I had to sit carefully and make sure that I didn't slam my head on the desk if I accidently fell asleep. My teachers had to give me extra help because I couldn't remember lessons from previous classes. Since I wasn't allowed to play my trumpet,

I watched and learned, wishing that I could play along with the other kids. Migraines would hit me from out of the blue and disable me for a class or two. Thunder roared inside of my head, making me nauseated and light sensitive. I couldn't hear or see anything but pain. It wouldn't stop until I took a nap and some painkillers.

My mom's depression, which she battled her entire life, would make her feel all alone even when she was around other people. Now I felt the same way. As the months dragged by, the skin on my face healed without any scars; only a little nick of my eyebrow was gone, and I could live with that. But with the physical proof of my trauma gone, people got more irritated when I repeated the same thing or told them I didn't remember something. And no matter how hard I tried, I couldn't remember what happened on the day of my accident. Nor could I remember much about my childhood.

■ ■ ■

After a year, the bones in my face were fully healed and I was no longer restricted from activities. But I was still cautious, still flinching at sudden movement around my face. I was a freshman starting at Shelby

County High School, with all new teachers, which meant that I had to explain what had happened to me, why my memory was so poor. It felt like a metal ball of nerves was sitting on my stomach. I'd never been good at one-on-one conversations with strangers. Feeling shy and awkward, I'd beat around the bush, glancing around the room while playing with one of my rings. I was embarrassed about my memory loss, and never told anyone about the accident unless absolutely necessary.

I had trouble in almost all my classes. I couldn't remember facts that I read in books, nor could I remember lessons. Lost information felt like it had fallen into a deep pit, never to be seen again. Tests felt like a huge waste of time, especially the ones that required me to write a whole paragraph on something that I couldn't remember learning in the first place. I started getting in trouble for little things, like not paying attention, which wasn't a case of being a poor student but of having a legitimate disability. Whenever I'd tell my teachers about the accident, they seemed to think I was lying or exaggerating. Eventually, I didn't bother trying to explain.

At home, Mom and I were closer than ever, even though we argued a lot.

We understood each other's pain. We read the same kinds of books and watched the same TV shows, mostly fantasy. The world of vampires, werewolves, witches, fairies, goblins, and black magic allowed us to escape our realities. We'd discuss the characters and plots for hours. Our favorite book series were J.R. Ward's *Black Dagger Brotherhood*, Laurell K. Hamilton's *Anita Blake: Vampire Hunter* and Richelle Mead's *Vampire Academy*.

I was barely passing my classes as I started my sophomore year, and then our landlord sold our house out from under us and we had to move. I switched to Eminence High School, and the cycle of having to explain my memory loss started all over again. Ironically, my teachers would often forget about my forgetfulness. My grades kept falling, and then, on a winter night, I slipped and fell on wet mud at school. I'd been playing in the band at a football game. It was just a little fall but my heart was pounding as I lay there on my hip. At home, I told my mother I was okay. But the morning after was a completely different story. I awoke with severe pain in my back and legs and could hardly walk.

After a couple of days of being absent from school, Mom took me to the chiro-practor and we learned that I didn't have the right spacing between my vertebrae. Apparently, when I hit the telephone pole, the blow caused my spine to get compacted. Pinched nerves in both legs from the fall. My back hurt, my knee hurt, and what did I eat yesterday? My body was falling apart along with my mind.

Nobody at school understood what was wrong with me as I limped around—they gave me weird looks. But my mom understood because she had a bad knee and a bad back from a previous injury. Only thirty-four, she knew what it was like to walk around and worry that the next step was going to bring you down for a week or longer. She was working as a security guard at an airport when she hurt her knee by stepping on an escalator the wrong way. She pinched nerves in her legs and had to relearn how to walk. There was nothing she talked about more often than chronic aches and pains, and now we compared notes.

■ ■ ■

In the middle of my sophomore year, we had to move yet again due to another landlord issue, and I switched to The Academy @ Shawnee, located in the West End of Louisville. When I walked the concrete paths outside the school, I was awed by the building's architecture and size. It reminded me of a castle, one that should have been in Ireland or Scotland, not Louisville. I chose to sign up for the aviation program, a pilot training curriculum unique to Shawnee. I thought it would be cool to be a pilot, but I quickly learned that the classes required a lot of memorization. On the first test, I realized how hard it was going to be for me. None of the questions were multiple-choice, so I couldn't even guess. I stared at the paper, flipping it over, pushing it away, pulling it close, until my head started to hurt.

The teacher wasn't happy with me. I wasn't happy with him, either. When he asked why my paper was blank, I told him that I couldn't remember any of the answers. I didn't say anything about the accident, even though I had become a blunt person when it came to my disability, a lot like my mother. He gave me a disbelieving look, and walked away with an irritated look on his face.

After school that day, I went to a guidance counselor and asked if she could transfer me out of aviation. We discussed my accident and how it was going to make completing the aviation program impossible. I doubted the teacher would make special

accommodations for me, and I was too proud to ask. The counselor transferred me into a gym class. Weightlifting, to be exact. My future switched from female pilot to female bodybuilder. But I liked getting dirty and loved gym, so why not give it a try?

At my first class, there was a herd of guys waiting to get into the weight room, all of them bigger and taller than me. When the door opened, the smell of sweat and metal hit me like a brick wall. The guys looked at me as I walked past them, their faces scrunched up in confusion. I knew what they were thinking. *How can this little girl be in here with the big guys? Will she even survive the first day? Will she quit when it gets too hard?*

The weightlifting teacher was taller and slightly bigger than the rest of the guys and had the attitude of, "Don't mess with me and I won't mess with you, but if you do mess with me, then you're the one who will be hurting." He called everyone to attention, his voice powerful and loud in the small room. It had a rubber-like floor with four sets of weights, flat benches and bars. The equipment looked big and intimidating. There was another machine that the teacher explained was for your legs and back, so those parts of your body could get stronger.

"Listen up!" he barked. "Before we start anything, I'm going to give you clear instructions. You need to know what each exercise is working in your body." He walked over to the flat benches and asked for a volunteer. A senior stepped forward and lay back on the bench. The teacher stood behind the bar, which weighed forty-five pounds. My eyes popped out. Forty-five pounds? On the first day?

The guy shook out his arms and wrapped his hands around the bar. Then he counted to three and pushed the bar up while the teacher spotted him. He slowly lowered the bar to his chest and slammed it back up in the air, as if it weighed nothing. Worry started to build inside me.

"If the weight is too much and you need help, yell out for your spotters," the teacher said.

We all scattered off to a bench and got to work. In my group, I was the first to go because we had to lower the rack so I could reach the bar. Taking a nervous breath, I put my hands up, wrapped my tiny hands around the cold metal, and squared my shoulders.

"One, two, three," I counted off, and my spotter lifted the bar and then let go, letting me feel the weight. Forty-five pounds felt like four hundred. Slowly and carefully, I lowered the bar until it touched my chest, and then struggled to push it up, my legs kicking out.

"Put your feet down," the teacher said as he walked past.

I did what I was told, and after a hard push, got the bar off my chest and racked the weight with the help of my spotter. Then I helped spot the other guys in my group. My arms felt tingly and useless, but I felt proud of myself, high on adrenaline. I went off to my next class feeling hard-to-concentrate wonderful.

I was better in weightlifting than any other class because it didn't require any memorization, just physical strength. Some days I moved around like a well-oiled machine, other days the machine started to rust, especially if I didn't stretch. In general, the class was helping me with all my aches and pains, almost like physical therapy. I found satisfaction in taking care of my body. It felt as if I was lifting the weight of my emotional life off my shoulders. Soon I began to make a few friends at Shawnee. My memory improved somewhat, but learning was still difficult and my past still foggy.

■ ■ ■

My memory remains foggy to this day. For example, I might hear a song and remember something random from years ago, like eating doughnut holes while listening to the same song. But I can't remember anything important, only disconnected fragments. I have good and bad days, which I put into four categories. One is my semi-functional day where I can focus, but not a lot. The second is where my nerves are eating at each other, making me on edge and jittery, like I ate a mountain of candy, and it's hard to write, sit in a chair, do anything. The third kind is the worst—I call them my wet blanket days. I feel like a soaking wet blanket has been thrown on me, and it gets heavier and heavier, making it hard to breathe, think, talk—the only thing I'm capable of is getting mad. But the fourth kind of day is perfect: I can focus and do what I need to do.

As I drag my pen across the paper writing this essay, I watch before my eyes a story being unfolded. Even before my accident, I loved writing stories, and I still want writing to be a part of my life. I've already written a fantasy novel. My imagination was not affected by the accident, and I am at my best filling the lines of an empty page. The world is at my fingertips. Writing stories makes me feel like I can be anyone and do anything. Even now, my head is rambling with plot ideas that people might

want to read. I see gargoyles flying down from the night sky and picking out a human to take back to their lair, and a human stumbling into a fantastical world that was not meant for him or her to see, and a vampire wanting to be a human again and doing anything it can to fulfill its wish. Being able to look at the world through different eyes is my talent, being able to look at characters as possibilities waiting to happen.

When I look at the eighteen-year-old girl in the mirror, I see my own possibilities, but sometimes the girl feels sad, angry, and frustrated. She isn't afraid to be herself and give her opinion on things, even if it ruffles feathers. The word "college" fills her with anxiety. It could mean a bright future, or it could mean academic setbacks, more explaining why her memory is poor, rehashing a painful story involving a four-wheeler and a telephone pole. The military is an option—I think I'd enjoy the physicality and structure of the training. Or maybe I could be an athletic trainer, or a physical therapist.

When I look at the girl in the mirror, I know she is strong and that she doesn't back down without a fight. I still see the scars, though they have healed on the surface, and I know for certain: as the years of my life move along, I will overcome whatever obstacles come my way. ■

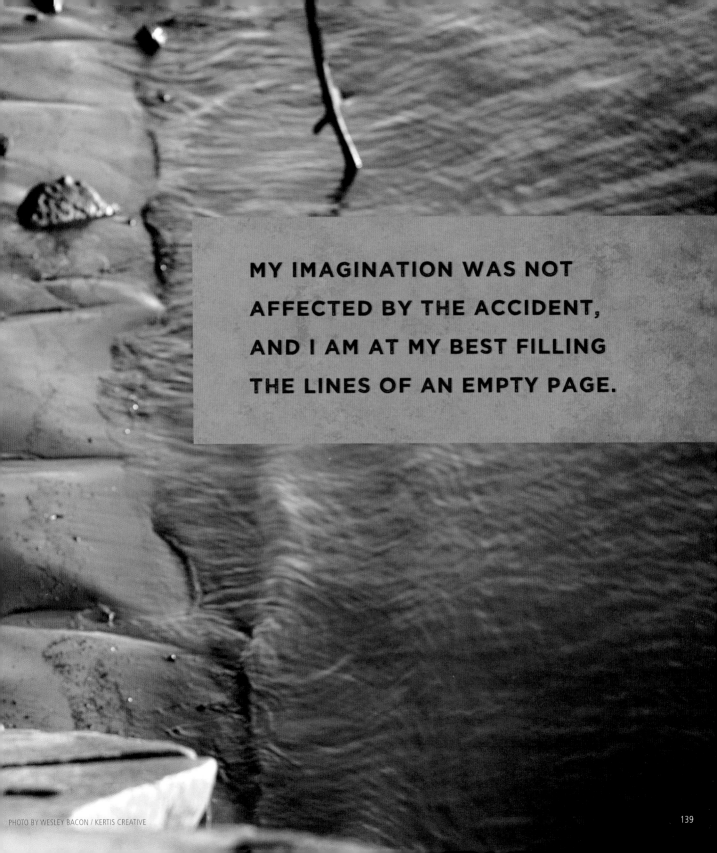

MY IMAGINATION WAS NOT
AFFECTED BY THE ACCIDENT,
AND I AM AT MY BEST FILLING
THE LINES OF AN EMPTY PAGE.

MUD PUDDLES

Carrie Winemiller is my motherboard; that's my nickname for Mom because she loves sci-fi. Yeah, she gets a kick out of it. She's not what most kids my age consider a "normal" parent. She says I'm not the typical teenager either, that being able to trust me to behave responsibly is a blessing. Can't say any of that describes the majority of mother-daughter relationships, but hey, that's what makes us special.

My older brother Lance and I are twenty-two months apart. Lance is autistic, making our ability to relate somewhat difficult. I look out for him as much as I can, and I know how to since we've been in a single-parent household more than half of our lives. I know that my mom needs help. In this interview, she and I talked about her parenting challenges.

CARRIE WINEMILLER:

Lance is different because of his autism. You and I have more of an average relationship. I won't say "normal" because I don't even believe in that word. I think everybody is normal. I think we're all unique and different. Lance doesn't have as much imagination as you have, but he's very intelligent. He's a history buff like you wouldn't believe. Ask him anything, and he knows it.

The Winemillers

When he was born, I could tell the difference immediately. He didn't like to be bathed. You couldn't touch him with water. He just screamed. A crowded area with people, a lot of noises, it would freak him out. He was very solitary. When he started crawling around, he would put himself in a position to where he was by himself all the time. One doctor said, "No, I don't think he's autistic," but didn't actually test him for it. He was tested after we moved back from Fresno to Elizabethtown in '06. He was about ten, and that's when everything fell together and made sense—why he was the way he was. And it made it so much easier, for me anyway.

When you were really young and we were living in North Carolina, we didn't usually have access to a vehicle, so we were pretty much home all the time. You weren't around other kids your age, and I didn't realize that you two needed to interact more with kids. I was like, "They're interacting with themselves. They're kids." I wasn't talking a whole lot at home and teaching you new words because I was the only adult. Your stepdad was working all the time.

I made a friend through a support group who happened to be a professional therapist, and on her first visit to our house she noticed that you were behind. I'd been at home with you for two years. You weren't growing the way that you needed to. You were behind in your speech and your motor skills. You and Lance had your own language. I couldn't understand a word of it. But that was fun; you had to interpret everything that he said for me. You two were cutting words off and flipping them around. You were doing your own thing with words. It's like what twins do sometimes. When Lance wouldn't say anything at all—it was just his body language or whatever—you knew what he wanted. A lot of times, it was like you could read his mind.

My friend suggested that I start getting professionals involved to try to help you guys out, so I did. At ages three and five, you started going to Head Start so you could be around kids your own age and learn to interact. I also got you into more therapy, vocational and speech and all this. Now Lance has got a vocabulary you just can't believe. He comes out with million-dollar words, and I have to ask him, "Lance, do you even know what that means?" He'll spill off the definition. I'm like, "Okay, fine."

I was such an OCD control freak when you two were young. My life was out of control, so I tried to control the things I could. At the time that I started getting you guys into therapy, they were therapying me. They said, "Just let them be kids. Let go." So I started letting go a little here, a little there. And one of the things they suggested was to let you guys get dirty. I started letting you play in mud puddles in your diapers as a way to let you just be kids and have fun.

The first time I consciously let you play in a mud puddle, it was hard. But it was so much fun. By the time you all were done you were completely covered and just smiling ear to ear. Another good thing was filling the bathtub with Jell-O or rice because it provided positive sensory input. So we started doing all kinds of fun things that ended up bringing out your personality like you wouldn't believe. It was very therapeutic for me to watch you go through that. You always loved to get muddy. ▪

ASIA FREY

Owen Street, Portland

Waiting for Tony

Teamwork

OWEN STREET, PORTLAND

During my childhood, most of my friends were boys because there weren't any girls living on my street who had the same interests as me. I was more into reading *Goosebumps* and *Harry Potter* than gossiping about boys. Most of all, I wanted to go on adventures, like the characters in my favorite books. My older brother Tony felt the same way, and one day when we were six and eight, we decided to dig for treasure in a corner of the back yard, using shovels that were taller than we were. I kept hoping we'd find something valuable, an artifact that would go to a museum, and we'd get credit for the discovery. We dug for a few days and didn't find anything, but it was still exciting.

Not long after that, I met a new friend on our street named Nick. The first time I saw him, my brother warned me to stay away from him because the two of them had gotten into a fight. Once school started back up, I was surprised to see him in the same class as me at Roosevelt-Perry Elementary. When we had a group project, I spoke to him, and found he was friendly. We ended up becoming best friends and traveled to school together every morning, sometimes on the school bus and sometimes getting a ride from my mom when she used to work at Norton Hospital.

Tony ended up becoming friends with Nick, too, and with his brother. We'd all play basketball in their back yard, which was small and had a lot of things piled on one side and covered with a light-blue tarp, things like a motorcycle, a ladder, old bike wheels, and mysterious pieces of rusty metal. I was way better than them in basketball back then.

Nick's bedroom had bunk beds, and a TV with Nintendo. It was our hangout, our clubhouse. We'd all play video games, and most of the time I won. I was competitive, and the boys would be moody after losing to a girl.

We'd also go to Boone Park, where there was a jungle gym and swing set. I'd usually go on the swings with my friend Brittney, who still likes swings to this day. My brother and Nick would play basketball on the asphalt court with other kids from around the neighborhood. I liked the park best around Christmas, when the big pine tree would be decorated in blue lights, the same color every year.

Across the street from the park was a small yellow store, and the owner allowed us to stay for as long as we wanted. There was a pinball machine and a claw-crane machine, the kind where you try to grab stuffed animals and other prizes. We'd play the games and share some food— popcorn, wings, pizza, nachos.

Those were happy days, being a kid on Owen Street. Life didn't seem as complicated as it does now. When I was thirteen, Nick's family moved away. I later heard that he got in trouble and went to jail. I still miss him. ∎

The lot where Nick's house used to be

Asia Frey

WAITING FOR TONY

It's in my hand once more, this kitchen knife. I grip the big black handle tightly. I don't want to use it. Just having it in my hand makes me sick in all the wrong places. My mind is twisted. I leave it under my pillow and walk to my mom's room.

I ask my mom, "Where's Tony going tonight?"

She looks away from the TV and responds, "Oh, you know your brother. He's spending the night at your uncle's house."

I stare at her. Earlier, the three of us had a nice spaghetti dinner with salad and garlic bread. But now that Tony has left, mother and daughter are vulnerable to our neighborhood. My older brother, the man of the house, is strong and can protect us. He was once on the high school football team. He did weightlifting. He and I would fight sometimes, and from that I know he can fight well. When he goes out into the night, on his own path, Mama and I have to look out for ourselves.

We stare at the screen that shows funny, stupid cartoons. Mainly SpongeBob. My mom is my best friend, like peanut butter to jelly. Because my brother is so loud and high-strung and I am the opposite—calmer—I'm easier to talk to and listen to. Mama has been diagnosed with bipolar disorder, and I can help her calm down when she's upset. Teenagers normally turn on their parents, blaming them for their unhappiness, which I never understood. When I was growing up, I would cry when people yelled at me, but my mom would talk kindly to me, so why wouldn't I talk kindly to her? She's been there raising me, helping me grow, so why should I keep anything from her? She's my mother, the only one I get.

■ ■ ■

I go into my room and peer under my pillow to check that the knife is still there, for when I go to sleep. Why am I resorting to this? Is the night really so dangerous? I have worries about what goes on with Tony. I worry that the house might be broken into.

I try to relax while Mama talks on the phone with friends and family members. They call with relationship gossip or recent news or to discuss what to do tomorrow. When I pass her room, she covers the phone's mouthpiece and says, "Hi." Sometimes they call as late as 4:00 a.m., startling us from our sleep, the phone's ring echoing through the house. My mom calls me "half-vampire" because when I can't sleep, which is often, I stay up all night listening to music and watching TV. The night is my world.

Right in the middle of one of my favorite songs, Mama shouts my nickname: "Dolly!"

I rush into her room. "Yes?"

She looks at me, half asleep. "Dolly, can you go into the kitchen and get me that big butcher knife in the kitchen drawer?"

I still remember the first time she asked me for that knife. She already kept a metal bat for protection. I thought she was a little crazy. I asked why in the world she needed a knife too, and she said, "So I can sleep. With Tony not here, there's no one in the back of the house."

When I was little, across from our house there was a blue house that in the daytime seemed normal, but at night had wild parties with loud music. I'd sit there with Tony, lights off in my pink-walled room, two identical pairs of brown eyes staring out the window, so curious about what adults do at night, not yet knowing

Mama and me

much about the adult world of disappointments and bad choices. We were little spies observing our target, until—what's that sound in the distance? Sirens. Police cars coming to break up the party, which sometimes meant arresting people.

But we live in a decent neighborhood. It has its moments when it wants to shine. Most of the people are nice, but you still have to be careful. We all look out for each other. If someone has to move something heavy, others offer assistance. If someone has a garage sale, my mom, brother, and I look around to see if we want anything. One time, we bought a shark cookie jar. When you opened the shark's mouth, it made the music from *Jaws* that tells you the shark is coming.

I tell myself that's the reason why I have a knife under my pillow. A shark might be coming. And my brother goes out sunup to sundown, without telling my mom and me where he goes or what he's getting into. He's probably out having a ball, living up the night in wild style. He often comes home late, talking on the phone with his friends, without even telling us, "Hello, I'm back home safe."

As a kid, Tony was accident prone. He had a dresser fall on him and break his nose. He fell off his bike and broke his arm badly, the bloody wound redder and wetter than the dry clay I'd seen at the Marchman Learning Center Daycare. A couple of years ago, he was in a terrible car accident. Every time he goes out, I imagine all the people who could hurt him and whomever he's with. I want to protect him, but all I can do is worry.

When I was seven years old and he was nine, at Thunder Over Louisville, I lost him in the crowd. I hated myself for not watching him more closely. I ran through the crowd looking for my mom so she could help. My eyes hurt from the tears, and then I became lightheaded. Finally, I found her and said, "Mama, I can't find Tony anywhere!" She looked at me and patted my hair down

to get me to calm down, and told me that he was with my cousin, Donald.

Now I worry that he'll get so caught up in his own life that he'll forget about Mama and me. What if I lost him as my brother? Or what if he does something that makes me not want to be around him? Maybe my biggest worry of all is that he'll turn out like our father.

■ ■ ■

My father is distant from me. I'm not being mean, but he just wasn't around much when I was younger. Now that I'm older, I don't wish to have a relationship with him. As long as I have my mother, who's always been there for me, I'm okay with it. There are plenty of other kids I know who don't have fathers, so it's not all that strange.

My father's first name is Tony, same as my brother, but I didn't know his name when I was really little. The first time my mom said that my brother and I were going to spend time with "Tony," I stared at her, deep in thought.

"Who's Tony?" I asked.

"Your father."

My mom left him when I was a baby because he was physically abusive to her. I didn't know that when I was a kid, though—I just knew that things hadn't worked out between them. Back in my elementary school days at Roosevelt-Perry, he would sometimes visit me in the hallway outside of class, saying he missed me, and that I should come and see him. We'd talk about lost time and new developments in my life, like when I joined Girl Scouts. He'd ask for visits, and I would agree. I was actually happy to see him, but I also didn't want to open myself up to him. He would buy me gifts to gain my affection. For one of my birthdays, I had three cakes: one from my mom, one from my father, and a third from somewhere else.

As my brother and I got a little older, we'd stay with our father for a few days at a time. He took us a lot of places, but I can't remember where, exactly, just vague memories of the basic structure of houses, what color they were. I felt out of place with the people he introduced us to; they were probably on his side of the family. They wanted to talk to me and act like they knew me, but they didn't.

Later, he got on house arrest, so he couldn't take us anywhere or come see me during school. When I was fifteen, he got me a cell phone so he could call me, or vice versa. I didn't like to use the phone, but

when we did talk, he'd ask me if I loved him. I'd respond, "Yes," and he would reply, "No, you don't," and I'd say, "Yes, I do." I'd feel so mad at him, mad that he expected me to love him more than I did, and that he seemed to think I was a selfish person for not being able to do that. I'd wish I had the power to jump through the phone and punch him in the gut and give him a good black eye. I do still love him, just not as much as he wants me to or as much as I did when I was younger. I don't see him that often anymore.

■ ■ ■

My granddaddy was way more of a father figure to Tony and me. His name was Julio Burden. He was Puerto Rican and he trained horses at Churchill Downs. He later worked at Ms. Bullock's farm out by Oxmoor, where he helped with the horses and raised chickens. When he drove his truck around Portland everybody knew him. No matter where he went, he saw someone he knew. He'd pull his truck over to talk to his friends.

He was funny and all the kids in our family loved him. He was like an older kid. One time at his house, my cousins, Tony, and I were upstairs talking and eating on the

Asia Frey

My grandfather working at Churchill Downs

158

carpet, dropping food and then hurrying to clean it before Granny found out. Suddenly, it sounded like a huge explosion went off. My heart skipped a beat. Granddaddy was laughing at the bottom of the stairs, holding an air horn.

I spent the night a million times at Granddaddy and Granny's house, and it was always fun. My brother and I barely spent any time at home in those days. We'd choose which rooms we wanted to stay in. Sometimes we'd have to stay in the same room, and he'd sleep on the floor and I got the bed. In the back of their house, there was a shed where Granddaddy kept his tools and his two dogs, a big bloodhound named Sancho, and a pitbull called Sammy. I liked Sammy the most, his friendly personality and droopy face. Sancho scared me a little.

In the morning, we'd usually eat leftovers from the night before, like ravioli or noodles. But one time I wanted a traditional breakfast, and Granddad suggested we cook it together. He got out two different kinds of sausage, along with the eggs, bacon, toast, and grape pop to drink. I cooked the basics, eggs and bacon, and constructed a monster sandwich with it—the best breakfast that I had ever had.

Granddaddy showed his love with food. If we wanted two different things, like a hotdog and a big bag of chips, Granny would want us to pick one thing, but he' say, "Eat both." He'd pick me up from school and take me to McDonald's, buy me as much as I cared to eat. Or he'd knock on our window in the morning, waking us up with breakfast in tow: pancakes, sausages, eggs, hash browns, orange juice.

When I was fourteen, Granddaddy had a motorcycle accident and had to have open heart surgery. Later, his heart gave out. He was only fifty-seven. He passed away the day after my fifteenth birthday and I was supposed to attend his wake the next day. It would've been my first wake ever. I couldn't bring myself to go.

■ ■ ■

My brother comes home after dawn with red-and-black Beats headphones hanging around his neck. He comes strolling into our mom's room, where she and I are in bed watching the movie *Rio*, and lies down flat across Mama's stomach.

"Get off me, you're heavy!" she complains, but I can tell she likes his show of affection.

His head is on my stomach. I feel relieved, but also a little annoyed. "Where have you been?" I ask.

He doesn't answer.

"Let's push him off the bed," I suggest to Mama, smiling.

Tony looks up and smiles back. "I dare you," he says, and moves to the foot of the bed.

We lie there listening to the song "I Wanna Party" playing on the TV. I'm able to let all the worry and anger go for now, because all of us are together. Nothing else matters. These are the kinds of moments I love most: togetherness and not a worry in the world. ■

PHOTO BY ASIA FREY

I'M ABLE TO LET ALL THE WORRY AND ANGER GO FOR NOW, BECAUSE ALL OF US ARE TOGETHER. NOTHING ELSE MATTERS.

TEAMWORK

LeighShannon Butler is my mother and best friend. She means the world to me. I interviewed her about her life experiences, and this is just some of what she told me.

LEIGHSHANNON BUTLER:

I was born and raised in Beecher Terrace, which is a housing project. Back then everybody knew your family. If you were doing anything you weren't supposed to do, Mom and Dad were going to know. And it was a lot of fun. It was all right. I went to a lot of free lunches, and played games at the community center, and learned how to do a lot of things. Took a cooking class at the learning center, and sewing, and knitting, and making key chains. Made a lot of friends.

When we lived in Beecher Terrace, we only had a two-bedroom apartment. So it was me, your Auntie Telisa, your Uncle George. We all slept in the same bedroom. We had bunk beds, and then one day, your uncle George fell out of the upper bunk, and because of that he got his own bed, a cot to sleep on. And then your Uncle Benitez arrived. And then a year after him, your Auntie Veneica arrived. So it was five of us in one room. I slept on the top bunk by myself. George and Benitez, they slept together in the same bed, and then your Auntie Telisa ended up having a baby, Antonio, when she was fifteen, and they slept together. And then Veneica, she ended up sleeping with Mom and Dad in the other bedroom.

I moved to Clarksdale when I was fourteen. When I was a teenager, Clarksdale was a fabulous place to live. It really was nice. It was just fun. You knew everybody in the housing project. You went to school with everybody. We went to the gym to watch the guys play basketball—that's when I started being more into boys. Now, I'd always been a tomboy. Loved football, basketball, boxing, track—just a sports fanatic. I always had my hair wild like a boy, wore tennis shoes, wore blue jeans. Hated stockings, hated skirts—I

had to dress up every week because we were in church a lot because my granddaddy was a preacher.

But when we lived up in Clarksdale, I came out of the tomboy and the first boy I liked was white, not black. That was unusual amongst my friends, especially living in the projects, because not too many white people lived in the projects. I tried to hide it from other people, but I really, really liked this boy. I told a friend of mine, Stephanie Thomas. And actually, she liked him, too. And, you know, it kind of trips me out because look at me now. I'm going to get married next year and it's to Jerry Prather, a white man. A wonderful man, my best friend, and the love of my life. Met Jerry in 2004 when I was working at Central State Hospital, and since then my life has changed for the better.

Two of the most beautiful times in my life happened when I was in Clarksdale: the times when I carried my children. That was something indescribable. You never know something can grow like that inside your body. And your body just changes, and you have a little person in there. And they're just kicking and moving and—it was so amazing.

But after I had you and your brother, Clarksdale went downhill. There were a lot more murders, a lot more fights. I bet you don't even remember, but one time, you and Tony were playing in the park, and two masked guys ran across the street. They had bandanas on their faces and they started kicking one of our neighbor's dogs. Then they pulled out a gun and ran up the stairs to the neighbor's apartment, and started shooting. The neighbor was up on the third floor screaming out his window at the top of his lungs, "Somebody call the police! Please, help us!" And he and the lady in the apartment jumped out of the third floor. He broke both legs and she broke her pelvic bone. I had to run to the park and grab you. We went to Mama's until things calmed down.

But even then, Clarksdale wasn't all bad. Every year the Pegasus Parade floats came through. We saw the floats before the parade even started. Oh, God, it was so great. Every year at five in the morning they brought the floats down Liberty Street all the way up to the beginning of Broadway, and they came all the way back down to 9th and Broadway. Every year, I would wake up early and watch the floats come through. And I still take you all.

Eventually, I wanted to get us out of the projects. They were tearing down Clarksdale anyway, and they were going to throw us

PHOTO COURTESY OF LEIGHSHANNNON BUTLER

Hard at work building our home

Building our home with Habitat volunteers

PHOTO COURTESY OF LEIGHSHANNNON BUTLER

just anywhere. And I said, "No, I'm not going just anywhere. I'm going to my own home, me and my children." I could have bought a house, but I decided that Habitat for Humanity was a better route to go. My mom was the first one in our family to get a Habitat home. She built a two-story house on 23rd and Madison. I don't know if it's still true or not, but I think we are probably the largest Habitat family because we've had four houses in the same family in Habitat—my two sisters have Habitat houses, too.

This was a fun project to do. Building your own house, putting in your own floor, your own carpet, how you want your rooms to be—nobody gets to pick that stuff but you. I loved every minute of it. Oh, baby, there were so many people who helped work on this house I can't

PHOTO COURTESY OF LEIGHSHANNON BUTLER

Our family

even name them all. A lot of their time and love went into this home. If we were to tear down the drywall, you'd see the names of everyone who worked on this house written on the wood underneath.

Life's not always easy, but with my wonderful family and my wonderful home, I feel truly blessed. I have bipolar disorder and major depression. So I kind of shift a lot. I scare you sometimes. I try not to do that, but you know I have a problem. You help me a lot. You and Jerry and Mama. You three. I really have a team with you three. You three help me. You come in my room at night, lie in my bed, eat a lot of pretzels. And watch TV. If I'm having a bad day, you're there for me. ◼

CODY HARRAL

WALTER AVENUE, IROQUOIS

THERE ISN'T AAA IN THE AIR

450 POUNDS OF COMPRESSED NITROGEN

WALTER AVENUE, IROQUOIS

Off of Taylor Boulevard, turn down Walter Avenue, where there's a bright blue convenience store called Clark. That's what I tell people coming to my house. You are now in Iroquois. You'll see folks sitting out on their porches. They've been through a lot of hardship and you can see it on their faces. They just want to relax and enjoy life, but they can't. They have to worry about their families and how they are going to eat. When you pass them, don't look at them for too long, because you don't want to be cussed for staring. It's just being polite.

My house is a small two-story, three-bedroom home that is a creamy white color. The paint has faded over time. The house shows its age and all that it has been through. I live on the first floor with my sister. My parents have the whole upstairs, which sounds like a lot, but really it's only one room. We all share one bathroom. It can get hectic when we're all trying to get ready in the morning. We also have a family room and a kitchen. A normal house for most people.

Down the street is Michael's house. He's only twenty-two and lives with his close friend, Brian, who is twenty-one. Michael is my adopted brother, in a sense. My parents haven't officially adopted him, but we took him in when he was sixteen and my parents raised him up as one of their own. He lived down the street but hated being there. He didn't move in with us, but we fed him and he spent almost all of his time with us. I couldn't have asked for a better big brother. I go over to Michael's almost every weekend and we try to catch up, even though both of us are really busy.

There is a thriving immigrant population in Iroquois. Across the street from our house lives a Cuban family, the nicest folks in the world. Their son has an orange Nissan 3000GT which he has fixed up, rivaling the 1968 Mustang that my dad and I restored.

Next to the Cuban family lives a friendly family with three young kids, and I always try to keep a watchful eye out for them, considering we have robberies and drug trafficking in the neighborhood. Terry's family lives a little further down the street. Terry is a forty year-old with more energy than anyone I ever met. He used to play sports with my best friend Tristen and me. Next to Terry lives Biker Dave. That's what all the kids call him because he rides a motorcycle that he built from scratch. It's insanely loud.

PHOTO BY COBY HARRAL

Our neighbor Katrina, who is the mother of Tristen, renovated her home and it looks incredible now. I love to spend time over there with Tristen, just because I feel so at home. Katrina is like my second mother. She's given me some of the best advice. No matter how far we grow apart geographically, Tristen and Katrina will always be family to me.

You may notice a few elderly couples out on their porches. They have seen this neighborhood fall into decline over the years. The residents used to be pretty well off. Now it's the exact opposite. The houses are hardly maintained. Some have plywood for windows. But everyone tries to do their best by keeping their grass trimmed and by picking up trash on the sidewalks. Maybe we're not able to change the whole look of the neighborhood, but we're doing our fair share to help.

There is a strong sense of community on Walter Avenue. People help each other out, and I couldn't have asked for a better place to live. I've grown up knowing about the challenges people face, especially when money is scarce, which has helped me learn not to judge people by their appearances. You never know what a person goes through in his or her life, and sometimes those challenges actually make for a better person. Other times, those challenges make people take desperate measures that don't do anyone any good.

As far as I'm concerned, I live in the best area of Louisville. ■

THERE ISN'T AAA IN THE AIR

Flying is freedom. As a pilot, you're like Superman. You can actually make yourself fly through the clouds, like kids imagine they're doing when they spread their arms out wide and whirl around a room. Up in the sky, it feels like you're in total control of everything—your life, your hopes and dreams, your passions—and you can block out the world and relax. It's just you and God up there in the clouds, being free. I would spend my whole life up there if I could.

The main reason I went to the Academy @ Shawnee for high school was to take advantage of their aviation program: free flying lessons, culminating in a private pilot's license. This would normally cost about $42,000. Shawnee is one of only a few schools in the nation where this kind of opportunity exists. But I had concerns about going to Shawnee when I

With my family at Homecoming

first started. As a freshman, I was going into a totally new environment, a school in the West End of Louisville, which is known for low test scores and arrests. I was coming from Whitefield Academy, a small private school in the East End. At Whitefield, there were only two black kids in my eighth grade class. My parents thought it would be better for me to go to a public school not only for the flying lessons, but so I could experience more diversity.

On my first day, I was so nervous. What were the teachers going to be like? How were the black students going to treat a white kid from a private school? Was I going to fit in?

As my dad drove me to the front of the school, I saw the aircraft hangar off to the side. There was a Cessna 172 twin-engine Beechcraft parked in the fenced area, and a huge 747 jet engine UPS had donated, waiting for service. I felt a surge of excitement, even though the aviation program wouldn't start for me until my sophomore year. That felt like an awfully long wait.

The gothic architecture of the school made it look like a castle that had been built in the sixteenth century. As I walked into the bustling lobby, Whitefield seemed like a great place to go back to, a small school where I knew every teacher. To my surprise, I wasn't the only white kid, but I felt outnumbered and out of place. Dickies Workwear was the style choice for most of the students, and unlike at Whitefield, most of the kids didn't get dropped off by parents but rode the bus. They also had their own slang, which I had to get used to.

I had no clue how to get to any of my classes, but was fortunate to have a teacher point me in the right direction to find my first period, which was English. I had always hated English, not because it was hard but because it seemed completely pointless to me. Not the best class to start with. During second period, I met a kid named Ben Bommorrito. A fellow freshman, he was talking about playing football for Shawnee.

Both of us went to talk to Coach Leasor, and we started practicing the very next day. There I was, a tiny, skin-and-bone kid at one hundred and twenty pounds, trying to play high school football. When I tried to tackle the star running back, I got crushed. I didn't quit, though. I had made a commitment to the team, and I loved the game of football. It was fun to me.

Meanwhile, I worked hard on schoolwork, getting high enough grades to put me at the top of the freshman class. Late in

September, our science teacher, Miss Zipper, talked to our class about joining a NASA program. Participants would be able to send an experiment on the Space Shuttle up to the International Space Station. But my mind was on the football game I had that week.

For the game, all of the teachers decided to come out and support us. Miss Zipper found my parents and talked to them about the NASA program. On our way home, my parents lectured me on how this experiment was now going to be my top priority and football came second. I was also doing ROTC, and I felt they had no right to dictate every priority in my life. But they wanted me to take advantage of every good opportunity that came my way, and because I hadn't turned eighteen yet, they had the final say.

At the first NASA meeting, I arrived in a slouchy mood. But then in walked Ashleigh Blair Keister, and the minute I laid eyes on her, I fell in love. She had long brown hair that fell just the right way down her shoulders, and deep brown eyes. She was the perfect height: when we hugged, her head rested right beneath my chin. Of course I didn't get to experience a hug the first couple of times we saw each other, but

it was worth the wait. I could tell by the way she spoke to others that she had a comforting personality and cared for people. To me, she was beautiful in every way imaginable, and suddenly I started to like this NASA program a little more.

The experiment we designed tested the effects that microgravity, or the lack of gravity in space, has on lactobacillus GG, which is a good kind of bacteria in our immune system. I was in charge of all the lab work: chemical experiments and mixing solutions. We worked through the fall and winter and into most of spring, and it was a challenge to complete the work in time for the launch in Florida. We rushed to get done, and then the launch was delayed. NASA often needs to delay launches because of weather and other factors. This meant we had to modify our time-sensitive experiment by mixing new solutions multiple times.

Finally, NASA was actually ready, and we sent our final experiment to Florida late in the school year, which meant that by the time we got our experiment back, we would have to work during summer vacation to process the results. While our experiment was on the International Space Station, we got some incredible news. Miss Herrick and

With Ashleigh on prom night

Miss Zipper, our sponsors for the program, informed us that we would be going to Washington D.C. to present our findings at the Smithsonian Air and Space museum on live television. Not only did we have to process our results, we had to plan our presentation.

The summer flew by, and then it was time for us to take off for D.C. We boarded the plane in the morning and arrived in Baltimore that afternoon. We had a train ride into D.C. I had never ridden a train before, and I enjoyed experiencing all the bumps, the humming of the wheels along the track, the melody of the train. The weather outside was bleak and grey, but the variety of people inside the car brightened my day. Unlike my first day at Shawnee, when I was overwhelmed by all the diversity, I felt curious. I overheard languages from all over the world. Surely some of the people were tourists, like us, anxious to see the U.S. capital for the first time.

The next morning, we went to the Air and Space Museum to listen to presentations by the other schools participating in the program. We were met there by Congressman John Yarmuth, and he was kind enough to talk to us for a short while about our experiment, and tell us what it was like to be a congressman in Washington. The presentations by the other fifteen schools stretched over two days, so we didn't get to see as much of the city as we had hoped. We were stuck at the museum watching the other schools present their pieces. But we still had a good time.

On the final night, after the teachers had gone to sleep, all of the guys snuck into the girls' room, and we played poker and talked for almost two hours. Ashleigh and I got a whole lot closer that night, lying on the bed together and telling each other how we felt about a relationship. We didn't start dating, but it was one step closer to that. Then I had to go back to my room so that

I wouldn't get in trouble. It wasn't until a few months later that Ashleigh and I would finally date for the first time.

When it was Shawnee's turn to present our experiment, I could barely stand on the stage because my knees were shaking so badly. Thank goodness I had flashcards for my part of the presentation. It felt like we were up there forever, but in reality it lasted only about ten minutes. It went great, and we all posed for a picture onstage. Then, still on a high, we walked to Union Station and boarded our train to go back to the Baltimore airport.

I knew that the NASA program was the best thing that could have happened to me at that point in my high school career. More valuable than football. I actually had fun learning about physics and biology, and I made a lot of new friends in the process.

I started the flying program my sophomore year and learned about the history of aviation. We had many quizzes and tests over the "fathers of aviation," both pilots and developers of new technology. We went on class field trips to Clark County Airport. The twenty or so students got to go up in a Cessna 172 and take control of the plane. Some of the kids threw up. We could tell who the true pilots in the program were!

Toward the end of the year, my progress toward becoming a pilot met a scheduling challenge. Mr. Cain, our aviation teacher, informed me that I wouldn't have time to do both aviation and ROTC the following year—the demands of the aviation program were going to intensify. The junior year of the aviation program covers the material on the FAA exam, and passing that exam was the only way I could fly with an instructor. But I didn't want to quit ROTC because it looks great on college applications, and I had fun doing it.

Mr. Cain offered me the opportunity to come during the summer and take the whole junior year curriculum in three weeks. That summer, I met Mr. Cain at school at eight in the morning, and along with four other students, crammed information for three hours a day. It was the most grueling and rewarding summer of my life. I would go home from class and study for hours so that I could pass the tests that I took the next day. I got very little sleep and had trouble staying awake in class. The final Friday, Mr. Cain gave us the final test to see if we were prepared to take the actual FAA exam at the airport. All five of us made the cut.

At the airport, I volunteered to take the test first so that I could get it over with. I was a nervous wreck waiting for it to start, and finished in fifteen minutes, which is a blazing speed—the test is supposed to be an hour long. When it came time to click the final answer, I paused. After the final question, the computer would tell me if I passed or failed. My flying future came down to this—would I pass or would I fail? I passed with a 75%, a decent score for having had only three weeks of preparation. I was especially proud to be the first student from Shawnee to complete the course as a sixteen year-old going into his junior year—it takes most students until their senior year.

Now it was time to start flying. My first instructor, Matt, reminded me a lot of myself: he liked sports and flying. He was the person who signed off for my first solo flight after I had logged twelve hours of flying with an instructor. I'll never forget that first solo flight. I felt extremely nervous but knew I'd be okay because Matt had taught me what I needed to know. I didn't really focus on the view of Louisville from the cockpit; I was focused on not crashing into another plane, and then landing safely.

Unfortunately, Matt couldn't keep instructing me because his other jobs were taking up almost all of his time. So he told me that I would start flying with Tyler, who

Up in the air above Louisville

was his good friend. Tyler and I flew almost thirty hours together; I could tell he was a great pilot, and he taught me all the stuff that I would need to pass the final FAA pilot test called the Check Ride. The test has two parts: an oral exam over a three-hour period, during which an FAA examiner asks you questions over anything and everything relating to airplanes and how they function. The examiner can ask you *anything* he or she wants, and you have very little room for error.

If you pass the oral portion, you can continue onto the flying portion. It involves all the maneuvers that keep you and your passengers safe. If there is little room for error on the oral portion, there is *no* room for error on the flying part. You could cost people their lives. As my aviation teacher at Shawnee, Mr. Cain, says, "There isn't AAA in the air; you can't just pull over in a cloud."

I took the Check Ride on Friday, July 19th, 2013. The week before, I went into the airport every day from eight to five and studied for the oral exam. My instructor was present during these study sessions, so I could ask him questions. I felt confident that I could pass the flying portion; it was the oral that worried me. I passed the oral test in two hours, pretty fast. I knew all the answers.

It was the flying portion that ended up being the more difficult part. It was one hundred and five degrees outside, and inside the plane it was a lot hotter, a metal furnace with no air conditioning. The examiner was a stern guy, but for good reason. Flying is no joke; safety is critical. I managed to fly my absolute best and passed with no worries or heartaches.

It was a huge relief to know that all the studying and hard work had paid off and I was officially a private pilot, the first junior to ever get his private pilot's license at Shawnee. This meant a great deal to me because I was helping lead the way for more kids to get their private licenses through the Academy @ Shawnee.

A lot has changed since my first day at Shawnee. I'm a college-bound senior, the starting quarterback on the football team, and a private pilot, one of only two in Jefferson County Public Schools. I've had opportunities at Shawnee that I never would've gotten at Whitefield. I've made friends with kids from a wide variety of backgrounds. I stepped out of my comfort zone, and Shawnee has prepared me for flying and the real world. I'll be ready for anything. ■

Cody Harral

I DIDN'T REALLY FOCUS ON THE VIEW OF LOUISVILLE FROM THE COCKPIT; I WAS FOCUSED ON NOT CRASHING INTO ANOTHER PLANE, AND THEN LANDING SAFELY.

450 POUNDS OF COMPRESSED NITROGEN

Michael Thompson is twenty-three years old and works at Louisville Industrial Supply. He grew up a few houses down from me, and currently lives in a different house in our neighborhood. Over the years, he has become a part of my family. He graduated from Iroquois High School in 2007, and from there he joined the United States Marine Corps, where he was trained as an artillery mechanic. From October 2009 through April 2010, he was deployed to the Helmand Province of Afghanistan. After that, he was stationed at Camp Lejeune in North Carolina, which is where this story took place.

MICHAEL THOMPSON:

You get three days off for the President's Day holiday. I decided to come home and see friends and family. I flew in, got picked up from the airport, went out to eat with my family, and then went to bed. Next morning, I get a phone call. It's my sergeant letting me know that one of my buddies and fellow Marines is in the emergency room and may not make it because he overdosed on drugs called bath salts. So they were doing a mandatory recall of the whole platoon. I wasn't home for twenty-four hours yet, and I already had to leave.

187

I got my flight rescheduled, which cost me $350, and then I flew back to North Carolina. I was driving to base when I received a call from my sergeant letting me know that I didn't have to come back yet. My buddy had come out of his coma and was doing all right. But I wasn't going to fly back to Louisville again. That was a Saturday, and then Sunday I didn't really do much on base, and then Monday, February 22, 2011, we were ordered by our commanding officer to disassemble a large artillery gun and reassemble it.

It was right after the weekend, everybody was tired, distressed, out of it. The CO wanted to know if we could do it in one day. The technical manual for that gun says that that procedure takes a minimum of four days. We told him that yes, we could do it, but everyone would have to work at my pace—I worked a little bit faster and knew more about the gun than my co-workers at the time. So we drained the equilibrators so we could remove the cannon tube, and then we removed the cannon tube. Then we removed the cradle from the body assembly, so basically the cradle was off the wheels, and then we were taking apart the accumulator. The guys that were working with me, I told them to drain the accumulator.

The cylinder is half nitrogen and half OHT, which is hydraulic fluid. They drained the OHT and thought they'd already drained the nitrogen, but they hadn't. So now we were trying to take apart a cylinder that was holding 450 pounds of compressed nitrogen, and we were taking the faceplate off, which stops the steel piston that's inside the cylinder from coming out. The housing has fifteen half-inch head bolts around it. We were on the last two, and they wouldn't come out. We couldn't figure out what was going on. The fact that it still had pressure didn't occur to anyone because everyone thought it was drained.

Most of the people were standing on the side of the cradle. I was up inside of it, which, with the stands and stuff, I think I was about four to five feet off the ground, right in front of where the steel piston would come out of the faceplate. People were prying on the accumulator, hitting it with a sledgehammer, shoving a screwdriver in there, cranking on the last two bolts. Well, one of the bolts finally broke and we're like, "Okay, there's one more bolt left."

This faceplate was right in front of my face and it just wasn't coming off. The guy to my left, he was cranking on the bolt with a ratchet. And then for some reason I was just

PHOTO COURTESY OF THE HARRAL FAMILY

Michael and Cody

like, "Well, I'm done with this," and I stood up, and I would say that I had time to stand up and turn slightly to my left before the cylinder exploded and the steel piston shot out and hit me in my right elbow, basically shattering it. Because of the percussion of the blast, I went airborne and landed about nine feet away.

The blast shook the entire maintenance building, the windows. I couldn't hear anything out of my right ear. The first thing that came to mind was like, "What the ---- just happened?" The next thought was, "Well, I've got to see if I'm missing anything." So while everyone else was running around panicking and stuff, I started to move my limbs to make sure they were all still there, they weren't broken, they were still working. So I started with my left arm, my left hand, and everything seemed fine. Then I did my left leg, left foot, and it was like, "All right." Then I got to my right arm and couldn't lift it off the ground. By this time, a sergeant was asking me if I was all right. I told him, "Well, I can't move my right arm, so I think it's broken."

I watched him as he reached over and picked up my right arm. My hand was palm up, and he pushed my head the other way, so I couldn't see anything when he turned my arm so the palm was down. I was like, "Well, I don't feel that, so I don't think it's broken." I figured there'd be pain. Then I turned my head back and saw my first sergeant—who is the highest command for our company on the enlisted side—running towards me as he ripped off his shirt. I just thought it was the weirdest thing in the world. I was like, "What, am I on *Baywatch* or something?"

I didn't know that I had a huge hole in my arm and was bleeding everywhere. My first sergeant used his shirt as a tourniquet, and a couple of other gunnies that were around pulled their belts off to stop the bleeding until they got some docs who were upstairs in the building to check me out. They said I was in shock. I kept trying to look at the wound, and they kept pushing my head the other way. I guess they thought I was in shock because I wasn't freaking out or screaming. I was telling them, "I just want to see what's going on over there. If a bone is sticking out, I want to see that. Or if my arm's gone, let me know. I've got to know what I'm dealing with."

All the staff and higher ups were in a circle around me, so all the people in my platoon and section had no idea if I was okay, alive or not. They didn't hear me screaming or anything. It wasn't until the ambulance arrived that I yelled to someone in my section to go into our break area and get my wallet because I needed my military ID before I could go to the hospital.

In the ambulance, one of the EMTs hooked me up to an IV, and the other guy was like, "All right, we're going to have to cut your coveralls off." I told him that that wasn't going to happen. The coveralls that I was wearing I got in Afghanistan. They meant something to me, and I'm a pretty short guy. It's very hard to find coveralls in my size. So I was like, "No, we're not cutting them." So to the EMTs' surprise, I wiggled out of a pair of coveralls with an IV connected to me and without the use my right arm.

I was in the ER probably four or five hours before they took me to surgery. I went up to surgery, met the doctors, was put under, and then I woke up. They said it was a success. I had a huge cast on my arm and was in the hospital for another two days. On the second day, I got a visit from the guy in our platoon who had OD'd. He was still in the hospital. He had apparently heard about what happened and wanted to see if I was okay.

They gave me forty-two days of convalescent leave. The bone healed all right, but now I have a titanium plate and eight screws in my elbow and forearm, and a very large scar. I also have a herniated forearm muscle, which, if you have ever seen *The Mummy*, looks like one of those beetles underneath my skin. ▪

Returning from Afghanistan

PRECIOUS BARNETT

North 19th Street, Portland /
South 20th Street, Algonquin

Surrender All

Purple for Peace

NORTH 19TH STREET, PORTLAND / SOUTH 20TH STREET, ALGONQUIN

When I was young, I would ask my mother what her neighborhood was like when she was a child and she would describe how every mother would watch for everyone's children, not just their own. She would always refer back to the old saying "It takes a village to raise a child." I experienced her old neighborhood every summer when I would stay with my granny for our summer break, and I stayed there for most of the past year.

The house is on 20th Street, right behind the Save-A-Lot on Dixie Highway. It's a street that I wouldn't have known existed if I hadn't visited her there my whole life. The street is narrow and the neighborhood is secretive, quiet. If you spot someone walking past who isn't a child of my generation, though, you can ask them how their day was and they will carry on a conversation with you.

PHOTO BY ASIA FREY

Corner store at 19th and Duncan

When I was a kid, I loved going over my granny's house, but I was used to crazy 19th and Duncan, in Portland, where I lived for most of my life. When we first moved there, it wasn't hard to get to know the people in our neighborhood because everyone was so open. If someone didn't recognize you, they would introduce themselves. It had a lot more activity than my granny's neighborhood, with lots of people out all the time and talking with each other.

Right next to the apartments I lived in is Boone's Park, the one park where Bloods and Crips don't mind being around each other. The guys play basketball, wishing they were playing for the NBA. Girls sit around the basketball court hoping that one of the sweaty guys will notice them. The kids have their own area where they climb on the jungle gyms.

Sign painted by Muhammad Ali's father, across the street from my granny's house

Growing up in Portland wasn't too bad. The place that really helped me and my friends stay out of trouble was The Portland Promise Center (PPC). PPC was a place where kids went after school to get help with homework and have fun without having to worry. PPC had people who were there in order to encourage and build up children. They had tutors and mentors. It was like a big family. If it wasn't for PPC, I wouldn't have ever been to Cedar Point, or gone camping or canoeing. Every holiday they would do something big for the kids such as giving us presents or parties. I remember one year I didn't show up to the center for months, but when Christmas came around they sent me a garbage bag full of toys. ■

Mural on the side of the Portland Promise Center

Precious Barnett

SURRENDER ALL

Even though it must have been really hard for my mother to have four kids to raise by the time she was twenty-one, she and my father were able to make my childhood a happy one. Thinking back, I see my father and me on a roller coaster at King's Island with tears of laughter in our eyes. I see the whole family in the living room laughing at a movie. Life was like a fairy tale. My parents were my superheroes, my brothers and sister were my closest friends, and money didn't seem like too much of a problem. Every Friday my parents would plan something different for the family to do for the night. Whether we went out to eat, went to the drive-in movies, or sat in the apartment and watched a movie, we were together.

As we all grew up, we started to dread being around each other. Simple questions such as "What should we do this Friday?" became small arguments. Eventually, our Fridays slipped away. My father started working longer hours. My older brothers and sister started spending more time with their friends. I began spending my Fridays in front of the apartment with my own friends. Without our family night, our relationships started to fade.

My brother Marcus was the one I would go to any time I wanted something and my parents didn't have it. When I was younger, I didn't know where he was getting the money—I just knew he had it. As I got older, I learned that he was selling drugs, and I started worrying about him. Sometimes he would get robbed, and sometimes he got locked up. Every time he was arrested, a girl in the neighborhood would open our front door and tell us the news. Each time I was scared that she would say that he had been murdered.

Our family stopped sitting and talking on the regular anymore. If we did, the conversation had to be brief, because otherwise someone was bound to cross a sensitive topic. The apartment became a battlefield that everyone tried to avoid. We started to stay in our own lanes. Now, when we came to one another, it was to say, "Look at what I have accomplished," or, "Hey, I need your help."

Although I went to church on Sundays, I started falling into the world and its everyday temptations. I never really went to parties or did anything outrageous, but my desires weren't the desires of a Christian young lady. I found myself getting into fights and trying to keep up with trends, wanting to be accepted by people, instead of by God. I also began to lie and argue with my mother. For about eight months during my tenth grade year, I smoked weed and even tried drinking liquor. All that ended when I got drunk for the first—and last—time, by drinking an entire bottle of E&J brandy. I decided that that wasn't the road for me.

I started to get a little more focused the following year. Track became a positive outlet for me, one of the few things that kept my mind off of all the drama around me. I would take my place on the blocks and pray as the man with the starting gun yelled my favorite words, "Runners, take your mark, set…" and *pow!,* the gun would go off. Left foot first, I would push my body with everything I had in me, my back still arched for the start of the race to gain speed for the 100 meter dash. After each race, I only had a short time to catch my breath, which left me with no time for my mind to wander. I ran the 100 and 200 meter dash, the 4x100 meter relay, and the 4x200 meter relay. While I was running, it would feel as if all of my problems stayed at the starting line. But I still hadn't managed to find a way to keep them there—I was constantly picking them back up as soon as the track meet was over. I would look out into the stands, and my parents wouldn't there, and I would get upset, wishing we had a stronger relationship.

■ ■ ■

The night was heavy; sleep was just around the corner. I was lying on my side on the floor and talking on the phone with my friend Reggie. I felt something slide against my leg. I looked down to find the hand of my brother's friend Stan. He moved his hand up my leg as I shook with fear. His face was cold and blank. Emotion no longer lived in his world. A strong scent of alcohol swept past my nose as he kept saying, "Get off the phone," slurring his words. In that moment, it seemed like Stan felt he had power over me, that he was in control of my life. My body rose along with my blood as I fought to be released. Then *boom!*, the door slammed shut and my brother ran up the stairs as usual. Stan jumped up faster than a rabbit and acted as if nothing happened. Terrified, I didn't tell anyone that night.

The next day I woke up feeling defeated. I wrote in my diary about what happened, and gave it to my mother. Telling her had the effect of both taking off and adding on pressure. I had gotten it off my chest, but now had to really face the fact that it had happened and that everyone would know.

After my mother read what I wrote, she told me to come to her room. She said she felt guilty because she wished that she could have protected me. She never wanted me to go through the pain that she once experienced.

The females in my family have a bad history of being hurt by people they trusted. My grandmother, mother, and sister were all raped at a young age. My mother was molested repeatedly between the ages of six and twelve and my sister was raped by someone she trusted at the age of ten. This three-generation pattern leaves me in great fear of being next in line. Although it has not happened to me, I don't trust men. It is hard for me to get close to others because I am always thinking about what may be going through their heads. The situation with Stan only made my trust issues worse.

After I told my mother about what happened, she asked me if I wanted to do something about it. I told her no. I was scared, and things seemed complicated. Stan was living with us because he was having issues at home and had just lost his father to gun violence. His father was a childhood friend of my mother's, so she felt obligated to take him in at this time of need. I called my aunt and asked her if I could stay with her for a while. Without hesitation, she said yes.

At my aunt and uncle's house out near Hurstbourne Lane, I felt more at home than ever. My aunt really tried to make me feel comfortable. She told me that I could stay in the computer room, where there were two beds, a computer, two couch chairs, and a television. I even had my own closet. She brought me a dresser for my clothes and treated me the same as her children, Kassidy and Jaylin. Staying with my aunt and uncle really took off a lot of pressure. I didn't worry about a thing. All I had to focus on was school, and activities of my choice, and my aunt and uncle pushed me to start really thinking about college, getting a driver's license, and things that would brighten my future.

■ ■ ■

It was 8:30 A.M. Kassidy, our friends Denise and Brooklyn, and I were tired from our sleepover the night before and were running around like headless chickens, trying to figure out what we were going to wear to church. Our spirits were high because it was the first time in about two years that all four of us friends had a sleepover together. When we got in the car, there was a debate about whether we were going to Sunday school or "big church."

Entering St. Stephen's Sunday school felt a little weird, because I had attended St. Stephen regularly for years, but had been going to a different church for the past two years. All that changed when I raised my hand to answer a question. All eyes rushed to me and several mouths yelled, "She's new! Give her extra Stephen Bucks!"

I was confused, but I accepted the bucks from a handsome brown-skinned guy, smiling in his light brown suit. He told me that with those bucks I could buy snacks from the church mini store. I smiled back and turned to Kassidy. "Who is *he?*"

"He is a minister here. I think they said he's twenty," she said.

He can't be! I thought. He looked fourteen, sixteen at the most. He grabbed the mic and asked the visitors to please stand. I looked around, wondering if I should move. I stayed seated.

When the class ended, Brooklyn told me that she was going to be with the young-looking guy. She thought he was cute, and that she had a chance, even though she was two years younger than me. I laughed at her and turned just in time to notice him approaching me. "Why didn't you stand when I asked the visitors to stand?" he asked.

St. Stephen Church

"Well, it's a little complicated. I've been going here since I was little. I just haven't been here lately."

"I've been here for two years and I haven't seen you."

"This isn't going to sound true, but during your two years being here, I started going to another church," I said, hoping he would believe the truth.

"Oh, okay. Well, I hope you continue to come."

"I will."

He looked at us all and thanked us for coming. Kassidy looked at me and said, "You like him, don't you?"

"Girl, he's cute, but I don't know him to like him. Plus I ain't going to do that in church."

St. Stephen's Family Life Center

Brooklyn looked at me. "I'm going to get him first."

A smirk came across my face, "Yep, okay, we'll see."

When the next Sunday came around, the only topic in the car was which of us was going to get the young minister. Sunday school ran smoothly that day. It was more of a conversation about the Bible than a lecture. After it ended, I walked up to the young minister and said, "I'm not a visitor anymore."

He looked at me with confusion, but then came that friendly smile again. "That's great!

Cecil

What's your name again?"

"Precious. And yours?"

"Cecil."

I laughed. "Like the street? A minister with the name of a gang-banging street. Wow."

He laughed too. "You're talking about my name now?"

"I tried to stop laughing. "No it's just…no, I'm not. Well, it was nice meeting you, Cecil."

We got each other's names, but it stopped at that. Later that day, I was on Facebook lying across the bed. I went to my notifications and saw that "Cecil Jesussoldier Clardy" had sent me a friend request. I got excited and ran into Kassidy's room and said, "Guess who wants to be my friend on Facebook?" She guessed it immediately. As the day went on, we went from writing on Facebook to talking on the phone.

I started to hang out with Cecil a lot, and we decided to be a couple. Most of our time was spent in the church or reading the Bible. My relationship with God was building, and I had found someone to share it with. Church, like track, was helping me to find peace. When my pastor, Rev. Dr. Kevin W. Cosby, was preaching, the messages always seemed like they were directed to me. As I listened to great preaching, and even more to the singing of the gospel, joy ran through my veins. It felt like an angel was touching me, letting me know that everything was okay and that God was on my side.

My uncle could see the change within me and decided that it was time for me to go back home to my mother. When I moved back, the apartment looked the same: dim lighting, off-white walls, mismatched furniture. The apartment reeked of a continuous rotation of cigarettes. But when I dropped my bags and headed to my mother's room, she greeted me with open arms and a warm smile. Time apart was just what we had needed.

I was happy to be home, but I didn't feel totally comfortable. I had a cozy bed at my aunt and uncle's house, but here I had to sleep on the floor. We had had to throw out my bed along with other furniture a while back when we had contracted bed bugs. When Cecil saw that I didn't have a bed, he insisted on getting one for me, but I couldn't let him do it. I turned his offer down. A few days later, however, he came to me with an air mattress, a pink sheet and a pillowcase, and told me that his mother bought them for me. He said there was no way he would take them back. I loved it.

Cecil helped me change my life and exposed me to Wednesday night Bible study. After a while, I stopped using my time at church to help me with my past, and began shifting to brightening my future. The sermons became clearer than ever, and on September 26, 2012, I was especially moved by a sermon titled "Surrender All." As I listened, joy ran through my veins, my body stiffened, and I felt tingling from my head down to my shoulders as if they were asleep. That Wednesday night I decided that it was time to fully give my life over to Christ. I decided to get baptized.

■ ■ ■

On the morning of my baptism, I woke up with butterflies fluttering in my stomach and sweat on my face. I was scared. I rushed to the shower and wondered what to do with my hair. I left it in a bushy ponytail and put on my clothes. I had the biggest smile on my face, but only to hide how nervous I was. This was going to be the biggest day of my life. After all the preparation of making sure everything was perfect, it was finally time.

I walked into the church through the doors closest to the baptism pool, rehearsing my line in my head as if it weren't a confession I have been dying to tell the world: "I confess that Jesus is the Christ and I accept him as my Lord and savior." The usher assisted all of the baptism candidates to the first row in the sanctuary. The lady on the stage called us up one after the other, reading off our written statements. When my turn was up, I froze, but my body was moving. The water crept up my leg as I walked down the stairs into the pool. It didn't stop rising until it was an inch away from my shoulders.

To my surprise, it was warm. I looked out into the crowd. St. Stephen is huge, almost like the mega churches you see on television. The bottom floor and the balcony were both filled with people. I have no idea how someone can go in front of this church to speak and not be nervous. It's like speaking to the whole world. I said my confession of faith, had my face dunked in the water, and took my place in the back of the pool as the next candidate faced the music. When all was done, we were guided to a back room, where the girls and boys were separated so that we could change into our dry clothes.

After I returned to the sanctuary fresh and renewed, I sat next to my family—my mother, father, Grandma Ann, Grandpa Jesse, my brother, my sister, my aunt, my uncle, my cousins, and even my mother's aunt Sherry. I still couldn't believe they were all there. That day felt like a dream. When church was over, everyone approached me. *I'm so proud of you. Your new life starts today. There is no going back from here. You made the right choice. Welcome to the church.* Everyone came welcoming me to a church that has always been my home. That day I introduced my parents to Cecil's parents. Everything was falling right into place. After leaving the church, my first stop was to O'Charley's

with Cecil, Kassidy, Denise, Jaylin, Aunt Elaine, Uncle Darryl, and Aunt Alicia. The day was perfect. I felt closer to my family and closer to God.

■ ■ ■

Life has not always been easy since I was baptized. I woke up one morning to find Stan sleeping on our couch, which made me feel angry toward my family and caused me to move back in with my aunt and uncle for a few months. Since I have been back home, things have sometimes been rough, but we are all fighting to better our relationships. My mother and I are able to hold conversations without getting into arguments. Marcus is no longer in the streets, has gotten a job and moved out on his own. My aunt and uncle take their time out to call and check on me to make sure I'm still on the right track or to inform me about different scholarship opportunities. My dad worked hard to make sure we could move into a house of our own. I'm still very active at St. Stephen, going to church regularly and singing in one of the choirs. There have been many times when I have doubted myself, and my future is uncertain, but I am learning to bounce back from challenges and trying my best to be the person I know I can be. ▨

SINCE I HAVE BEEN BACK HOME,
THINGS HAVE SOMETIMES BEEN
ROUGH, BUT WE ARE ALL FIGHTING
TO BETTER OUR RELATIONSHIPS.

PURPLE
FOR PEACE

He walks with a confidence that no one can break. He could care less what you think of him; however, he will treat you like you're the only person in the world. He is a walking music note. His words flow like water. He is my twenty-year-old brother, Kevin Barnett. To others, he is the kid who raps, but to me he is a hero chained.

KEVIN BARNETT:

I think the reason I'm not in the streets is because I have seen many, many people get murdered. People I grew up with. Since I started high school, I think there have been thirteen people that I knew personally—for years, at least seven years each—get murdered.

I had one cousin killed in a shootout on my mama's side, then a cousin killed in a shootout on my daddy's side. A couple of years later, my cousin got shot in the head. I just heard yesterday, another cousin was just shot in the car with her boyfriend. My uncle was murdered on New Year's Day 2009. It's wild. People are just being taken out. The streets aren't anything I want to do.

When I was younger, I didn't think the way I do now. Back then, it was just like, "Damn, they killed dude." I didn't follow up. I didn't know what the story was. I just knew that he got murdered. But now, like Dante Newsome just got killed and Charles Fambrough just got killed. I still see their sisters and their girlfriends and all that. It trips me out when I think, "Dang, I used to walk the school hallways with these dudes." And I can vividly remember their personalities, because I interacted with them on a daily basis. Every time he saw me, Dante called me Long Hair Don't Care. When he died, he was just now growing his dreads. His dreads weren't even long yet. We would always be in class talking about something that neither of us was ever going to do, some old silly stuff.

And Fambrough, the dude that died on Portland, didn't ever talk. He talked, but he would always say something weird. He would sound like South Park. But he would hoop. When we were in gym class, he would play basketball real hard. I mean, he wasn't that good, but if he had practiced enough to develop skills, he would have been a good basketball player because he wanted to win. He played hard.

I was by the park when Bibby got shot, Jermaine Bibbs. I had been in the park, but I had left, and I was in front of the apartment building. And I could actually see down the street, right down the street, as they hopped out the car and shot him up and then hopped back in the car and left. I had just left the basketball court. I had been sitting right on the wall right where they got shot. I could have been hit.

I've got a joke—I say that people start dying when it gets hot outside, because the heat makes people mad. But there really isn't any reason. I don't know. The economy. People want money. I don't know what it is that makes people kill other people. It's hard for me to get mad enough to fight somebody, so it's hard for me understand somebody getting so mad that they would go kill somebody.

I had a young friend tell me, "I know what I'm doing. I've come to terms with the consequences. I'm either going to die or get locked up." I said that was the realest thing I had ever heard. It was also the dumbest thing I ever heard, but it was the truth. He just figures that one of those outcomes is an inevitability. He feels like this is real comfortable, and it's easy for him, so he lives it like that because he's got to die eventually.

A lot of people's problem is image and reputation when it comes down to a beef, like, "This man disrespected me." When you take on the image and the reputation of a street person, you can't let that happen, because to people that don't have anything, reputation is everything. So if you feel like a person disrespected you, you have to address that.

I learned more from examples than anything. When I look at stuff that goes on, it makes me not want to do a lot of the stuff that I see gets people into trouble. I've seen so many things go wrong and so many things go right, and I can pick what path I want to take.

God is in all people. And there's good in everybody, and there's always a brighter side to every situation you could be put in. I've always been taught that everything happens for a reason, and you're on a path. So I just figure whatever happens to me, good or bad, it probably was going to happen. But I have to figure out *why* it happened. I can't be mad that it happened. You got to be analytical about the situation that you're going through. Sit back and ask, "Why did it happen like this? Why was this the result?"

Like a scientist. When you do experiments, half of learning is experience, the stuff you go through. So I figure you can't get mad about stuff you can't control. And if you can control it, then you would change it if you didn't like it. So there's never been a reason to be mad. I might get frustrated, because of human stuff. But I never let anybody make me mad enough to kill them. That's just crazy.

I've got a real positive outlook on life. I'm always happy, and somebody might be having a bad day and be annoyed at me. And I think, "You're mad at me because I'm *happy?*" I had a person ask me, "Why are you always smiling?" That doesn't even make any sense. Why are *you* always *mad?* My explanation is probably going to be shorter than yours, but it's going to be better. You've probably got a long story for why you're mad. I'm happy because I'm alive.

I've got plans to start a nonprofit organization, Purple for Peace. I want to lower the murder rate. But when it comes to nonprofit organizations, you've got to figure out how you're going to raise money, where you're going to have your fundraisers, what types of events you're going to have, whether or not you're going to walk, jog, have cookouts, family fun days. The good thing about having a nonprofit organization is that if you do the right paperwork, you can probably go in and get grants and loans and stuff like that from the government. But you still need the ideas. You can't just go and say, "I want this." You've got to have it set already, your plan all the way through.

I know that I'm able to do great things. The worst thing in life is to waste it. What if I was sent here, and I never found out that I can do great things? Like what if I was that kid with the bad perspective that sat in the hood and figured, "I am a product of my environment. I am this. I walk outside. I am the drug dealers on the block. I'm the baby mamas with no baby daddies, pushing a stroller with two kids sitting on each other's laps in the store that never has anything in it. I'm that. I am that because that is what developed my sense of what I am." But I know I'm greatness. When things grow, they grow from the bottom. And the top of whatever grows is at a different level than where it started. And that's what life is all about: getting to another level. You don't want to be on the ground. I want to be a tree, not a carrot. Carrots are in the ground, and I don't want to be a carrot. I want to be a tree. ■

ACKNOWLEDGMENTS

This book was truly a community effort, and as such, requires a rather lengthy list of acknowledgments.

First and foremost, our deepest thanks to the families and family friends of our authors—the Barnetts, the Cottons, the Freys, the Harrals, the McConicos, the Thomases, the Urbinas, and the Winemillers. Their loving encouragement and willingness to be interviewed helped each author in doing his or her work for this project.

This book would not exist without the generous financial support of many organizations and individuals. Special thanks to Chris Stokes and Vernon Robertson Urban Charities, Nick Simon and Publishers Printing Company, Gill Holland and Augusta Brown Holland, John Bajandas and the Arthur K. Smith Family Foundation, Mary Gwen Wheeler and David Jones, Jr., and The Lauren K. Weinberg Fund at Blue Grass Community Foundation.

To Keith Look, former Principal of The Academy @ Shawnee, for being such a brilliant catalyst, and for invaluable ongoing advice and assistance.

To the faculty and staff of The Academy @ Shawnee, especially Cecilia Omdal (for going above and beyond in helping us navigate all manner of challenges as our primary point person at the Academy), Danita Lewis (for lending us her classroom), Stephanie Conrad (for sharing her library with us), Dee Hawkins (for trusting us at the beginning), Jessica Dueñas Erickson (for being such an inspiring advocate for her students), James Rhodes (for having our back during our summer workshops), and current principal Houston Barber (for embracing this project so quickly after arriving).

To Joe Manning, for helping to lay the foundation with his enthusiasm, wisdom, sensitivity, and time, and for his invaluable contributions as one of our summer instructors.

To Jennie Jean Davidson, Dana Jackson, Althea Dryden, and all the good folks at the Network Center for Community Change, for showing us what community looks like, and for their invaluable partnership.

To Stephen Kertis, Wesley Bacon, and everyone else at Kertis Creative, whose stunning photography and video production helped make this project classier than we could have ever hoped for.

To Abram Himelstein of The Neighborhood Story Project in New Orleans, for his initial inspiration and guidance.

To Nikky Finney, who drove over from Lexington to lend her unforgettable presence to one of our class sessions, and to our local volunteer instructors who visited class or took students out in the field to take photographs: Anne Marshall Chalmers, Matt Frassica, Keith Williams, Adam Creech, and Claire Krueger.

To the posSOUPbility crew, for giving us an opportunity to gain some grassroots support at the very beginning.

To Shellee Marie Jones, for her tremendous book design, and for her patience in helping us crystallize a vision that would honor the authors' stories. And to other designers who have lent their talents to LSP: Matt Dobson, Carrie Neumayer, and Richard Rodriguez.

To Harold Weinberg, for his top-notch legal assistance during the pre-project formation of the Louisville Story Program.

To Cheri Bryant Hamilton, Anthony Smith, Imani Beverly, Jonathan Bastian, Kate Busch, Stephanie Brothers, Kent Thompson, Kyle Coma-Thompson, and The Green Building for their contributions to our first public moment, our Kickstarter launch party.

To Sarah-Jane Poindexter and Tracy K'Meyer of The Oral History Center at University of Louisville, where audio recordings and transcripts of interviews from this project will be archived.

To Merle Bachman at Spalding University for arranging a campus tour and writing workshop for our authors, and to Makalani Bandele for teaching that day.

To Carrie Neumayer and Lee Ann Massey for their loving encouragement and understanding throughout this project.

To all of the individuals who backed our Kickstarter campaign or made donations in other ways, particularly Phil and Landis Thompson, Madonna Badger, Susan Bentley, Joan Musselman, David Kaplan, Keith Look, Jonathan G. Lowe, Kristen Lucas, Duncan and Carol Taylor, Richard and Corie Neumayer, Chenoweth and Tyler Allen, Yanay Feria, Claudia Gentile, John Musselman, Roy Elis, Taylor Antrim, Jennie Cole, Rosalind Heinz, Thomas Nord, Ozair M. Shariff, Monique Ayotte-Hoeltzel, Jared Busch, Kyle and Marie Coma-Thompson, Elizabeth Cox, Fred Look, D.M.D., Judy Look, Katherine Mapother, Christy L. Rhodes, Andrew Sokatch and Rachal Aronson, Kent Thompson, Amy Washburn, Melissa and Chip Welsh, and Pamela A. Zipper.

And to the many other incredible people whom we just don't have space enough to thank. We are so grateful for every single one of you.